Tea Witchcraft

Over 160 Recipes to Prepare Magic Brews
for Love, Protection, Divination, and Healing.
Change Your Life with the Power of Herbs!
BONUS: 75 Tasseography Symbols and Meanings.

ALYSSA VERA

Proofread and edited by Amber Fritz-Hewer
Book Cover design by Teresa Monreal

About the Author

Alyssa Vera is a practitioner and author of guides about magic, spirituality, mythology, symbolism, and ancient beliefs. She firmly believes that magic lives within each of us.

Her mission in life is to inspire people to achieve their dreams by unlocking the magical abilities that all of us carry within and approaching the form of spirituality that better suits one's inner self.

Passionate about the different magical arts since she was a teenager, Alyssa has been dedicated to the mystical, magical and spiritual for nearly twenty years. Using her long history as a practitioner, she has decided to turn her knowledge into books and guides that can teach, in a practical yet comprehensive way, how each individual can bring out the best in themselves and the world around them through the most effective magical and traditional practices.

In short, Alyssa Vera's books are the perfect starting point if you are looking to discover all the magical and spiritual potential hidden inside of you and achieve the life you have always dreamed of.

You are invited to discover the other magical guides she has available on Amazon:

@witchcraftbyalyssavera

My Gifts for You:

Free Ebook – Value: **~~$ 12.99~~**
Spells & Rituals Printable Template: **~~$ 2.49~~**

To say **thank you** for buying this guide, I would like to offer you two little magical gifts:

1. My **ebook**: "**Crystals for Beginners**: THE 101 GUIDE TO DISCOVER THE POWER OF CRYSTALS FOR HEALING, MEDITATION, AND MAGIC. BONUS: 50 STONES DIRECTORY AND 11 EVERYDAY RITUALS." More than **100 pages** of information.

Find the Right Crystals for YOU and Achieve Mental, Physical, and Spiritual Harmony!

2. My **Spells & Rituals Printable Template**.

Keep Your Magic Well Organized by Recording All the Details of Your Spellwork!

Improve your life with the powers of crystals and keep track of all your rituals with these magical gifts!

Just Scan the QR Code with Your Phone:

Table of Contents

PART I

TEA WITCHCRAFT

Introduction

For centuries men and women around the world have been using tea for a great variety of reasons: to lower cholesterol, to recover from a cold, to alleviate stress, for meditation, and so on.

However, very few modern witches are fully aware of the great potential of tea witchcraft. And so little information can be found about tea for spells, treating chakras, divination, color healing, and all sorts of rituals.

And to me, that's truly a shame. In my experience, tea can really help change someone's life for the better, and it offers a highly effective way to use energy to achieve higher goals. That's why this powerful (and delicious!) tool shouldn't be missing from your magical repertoire.

Furthermore, as you will see in the upcoming pages of this book, it can be effortless and fun to work with tea and the different herbs. You don't need to be an expert herbalist to improve your existence with tea magic, and it doesn't even matter what kind of witch you are - tea rituals can be incorporated into all sorts of magical practices.

Even though growing your own ingredients and having full control over the power and the quality of your herbs is an advantage, you don't need to have a garden or the time to do such a thing. Tea witchcraft is accessible to all witches and offers easy alternatives for everyone willing or even just curious to start practicing.

Above all, making tea is and always will be a mindful process. And it can help you to fully understand who you are as a witch, bringing you inward to the very core of your magical practices. Just keep in mind that acknowledging the power of plants and recognizing that they have their own spirit is the first step to getting in tune with their magical powers and using them to achieve your dreams.

In short, practicing tea witchcraft is about mingling your energy with that of different plants, forming a bond that is considered highly powerful in magic and that can affect your body and spirit in all sorts of positive ways. This is a beautiful and surprising journey, and I'm beyond honored that you have decided to take it with me.

So, shall we begin?

Tea: a Little Bit of History

As you probably already know, tea is the second most consumed beverage in the world after water. It has been drunk for thousands of years, and its consumption has spread to almost every country worldwide.

One of the most widespread Chinese legends explains that the custom of soaking tea leaves in boiled water first started in China around 250 BC. Emperor Shen-Nung discovered this kind of beverage accidentally when he was boiling water in the shade of a huge tree. Some leaves fell into the emperor's pot; he drank the resulting infusion, and... the rest is history.

During the Tang Dynasty, this beverage ceased to be considered mainly a medicinal tonic, and its consumption for pleasure began to spread. Tea acquired such importance in this time that a group of merchants commissioned the writer Lu Yu to write the first and most important book on tea, "Su Cha-Ching," known as the "Sacred Book of Tea."

Before the word "tea" in English started being used and recognized worldwide, this magical beverage was given a variety of names: tcha, cha, cha, tay, tee, etc. The English word does not arise from the Mandarin Chinese "Tcha" but from the Amoy dialect. This is because the first contact between the Dutch and Chinese traders took place in the port of Amoy, in the province of Fujian. The name was then translated to "thee" in Dutch, and it spread to English-speaking countries from there, since it was Dutch merchants that first to brought tea to the Europe.

Antioxidant, depurative, digestive, rich in sodium, fluorine, vitamins, and minerals - the health benefits that science has found in this beverage are pretty impressive and vary somewhat depending on the specific range of tea, even though most studies have been carried out on green tea. However, it is generally understood that tea can boost the immune system and assist the body in protecting and recovering in case of viruses or infections. Some studies even discuss improvements in diseases that degenerate cognitive abilities, such as Parkinson's or Alzheimer's, and they stress the importance of tea's free-radical scavenger activity.

The great variety of tea available worldwide is also quite impressive - more than 3,000 varieties exist! This is because Chinese green tea and Japanese green tea, for example, would be considered two different teas, as their harvesting times and mode of preparation are not exactly the same. Thankfully these sorts of differences aren't anything you have to worry about because, as we will see in the upcoming pages of this book, knowing the main characteristics of the most common tea varieties is more than enough for your tea witchcraft practice.

So, precisely what does this century-old drink have to do with magic?

Tea Magic Overview

Even though tea has been used to treat diseases in China for hundreds of years, has been utilized for magical purposes, and, of course, has always been tasting great, tea witchcraft, also known as tea magic, is only just starting to receive some of the attention it deserves. And it was about time, considering that, with just a few simple tea recipes and the proper knowledge, tea can lift your spirits, give you energy and power, heal minor ailments, and add a little magic to your life.

If you think about it, when done with the right intent and attention, even the smallest acts can work powerful magic. A doodle on a notepad can become a sigil; lighting a candle can turn into a spell... and preparing a specific cup of tea can be witchcraft too. In other words, this seemingly simple form of magic perfectly exemplifies how a little effort can bring enchantment out of the most common daily rituals.

Tea witchcraft is both easy and accessible to practically everyone, allowing us to create magic in any setting. In fact, as previously mentioned, it can be used in a great variety of practices: from casting spells to divination, enhancing rituals, reading leaves, altar work, and much more.

In other words, tea is a must-have for any witch's cupboard, regardless of their specific kind of magic. If you think about it...what could be more enchanting than pouring hot water over earthy materials to create a powerful elixir? So, take some time for yourself and sit down with your favorite cup of tea. We are about to discover how you can use tea witchcraft to accomplish your goals and desires, and even the best recipes to increase the effectiveness of your magic.

So be ready and... believe.

Reading Tea Leaves

Am I wrong, or when reading about witchcraft and tea, was this the first thing that came to your mind? Reading tea leaves, also known as tasseography, is a type of divination that involves interpreting the patterns left in a teacup after the tea has been consumed. This method of divination dates back to the 17th century, shortly after tea was introduced to Europe. Some tea leaf readers use specialized teacups, but you may read tea leaves simply with a standard one from your kitchen. Just don't use a coffee mug because the curvature makes the process difficult.

Overall, reading tea leaves is a straightforward procedure. We will talk about it in more detail in the upcoming pages, but for the moment, here are the basic steps:

- Fill your cup halfway with hot water before adding loose tea leaves.
- Allow the tea to steep to your liking before consuming it as usual. (Some witches recommend drinking tea without milk or sugar, but I haven't noticed a significant difference in my results.)
- Make sure you have dregs remaining and enough liquid to stir the tea leaves but not so much that they fall out of the cup when it's overturned.
- Place a napkin on the saucer, swirl the cup three times and turn it upside down when you're done drinking your tea.
    - It may take a bit of practice to figure this out, but it isn't hard once you've gotten used to it.
- At this point, you can finally decipher the shapes and symbols left in the tea leaves by turning the cup right side up!

How? There are several ways to interpret the leaves left in your cup, and everything from the direction your cup handle faces to the height of the leaves on the cup's side can have an impact. If you're curious about this type of divination, don't worry, you'll discover much more about it in the chapter on tasseography.

Making Custom Tea Blends

Generally, pre-made tea mixes are created with taste in mind, but you can also make your own tea blend focusing specifically on your magical goal. Making homemade potions and spells is as simple as combining herbs for their magical powers and brewing them into teas.

And you can create your own library of magical herbal tea recipes and use it to cast a wide range of spells. In the upcoming chapters, I'll share some of my favorite recipes and all the correspondences you should know to help you create your own magical beverages.

Including Tea Witchcraft into Other Aspects of Your Life

Even though many people worldwide truly enjoy drinking tea, you might not be one of them. If that's the case, don't worry. There are still ways to incorporate tea and herbs into your magical practices without actually drinking tea.

Tea can be the base of your food recipes as a substitute for water. In many circumstances, a weakly brewed tea can replace water without significantly altering the taste of your food. You can even use a cold infusion if the meal you're cooking has a light flavor. For a cold infusion, simply place your herbs in the proper amount of cold water and then put it in the fridge for an hour. This allows the plants' energy to infuse the water without overwhelming the flavor. Just be careful, despite cold steeping, stronger flavors like citrus and ginger will most likely come through in the water. This means it's better to avoid these ingredients if you want your infusion to be as tasteless as possible.

Another great way to incorporate tea magic in your daily life is adding tea to your baths; it's an amazing method to upgrade the enchantment of your self-care routine. For this approach, you can use boh cold or hot infusions, and you can mix herbs that you might not ordinarily combine. In fact, because you'll be bathing in it rather than sipping it, your tea blends can be the exact magical concoction you need with no worrying about unpleasant flavor combos!
Overall, I suggest making a large batch of tea for baths; I usually use 1/2 – 1 cup of herbs and around 8 cups of boiling water. Steep the herbs in the water until the latter mixture reaches a comfortable temperature (it may take about 20-30 minutes, depending on the season). Strain your herbs and add the resulting infusion to the your bath.

Of course, using the right ingredients is essential to achieve the goal of your magical bath. And setting your intention is pretty important, since it helps your magic work more effectively and allows you to manifest your dreams. So don't forget about brewing your bath tea with intention.

Tea can also be used at your altar. This is because tea as an offering is a simple way to honor a spirit or deity, and there are various ways to do such thing. You can choose herbs that you love and make a cup of tea for them once or twice a week. (You can even boil a cup for yourself and drink the tea with them!).

Over time you may find this a successful approach to getting to know and feeling connected with the key spirits in your life. However, always remember that not all spirits like or want tea. Some of them might be wine lovers or just prefer some other beverage. At the same time, you should also find out how the spirits you are turning to like to drink their tea. So, just as you would do with a friend or relative, ask them if they want milk or sugar in it. You can also choose to offer your deities teas that go in hand with their specific preferences, rather than your own preferences or magical goals. We will talk about how to find out all possible information in the upcoming pages.

Scrying is another way to use tea on your altar. As you probably already know, scrying with simple water is a popular form of divination, but it's also possible to use different kinds of liquids. So, if you have a particular subject in mind for scrying, you can make a tea with herbs associated with that intention and utilize it instead of water in your bowl. However, be cautious about which herbs you use since certain ones with extremely high energies may skew the messages that are provided to you. This is why you should stick with plants that generally have light energy.

Potions, Teas, and Infusions

At this point, I would like to help you understand the main differences between potions, teas, and infusions. You may be asking, *Isn't it all the same?* Well, not exactly.

A magic potion is a method of attaching a tangible sensation, like taste or scent, to an idea, the goal you're trying to achieve. And teas and tisanes can be used to make a magical potion or, in other words, to give your prayer greater power. Whether you plan to drink the potion or not will determine the types of ingredients (only non-toxic if the potion will be consumed) and the kind of liquid to use: water, alcohol, or oil, for example.

In other words, a magic potion is something you can make when practicing magic, and teas and tisanes (non-tea-leaf herbal teas), as well as fruits, herbs, and spices, can all be ingredients in a magic potion, depending on the properties of each item and the purpose of the potion. Selection of the ingredients for a brew makes it simpler to connect with your wish or magical work by having you physically create something while your mind focuses on the goal.

Love teas are often are called potions. This is because floral and fruity teas are ideal for inducing feelings of love. Most ingredients in a love potion have been related to love for centuries and are considered aphrodisiacs. Women in some parts of the Middle East were even forbidden to consume red hibiscus tea because it is an effective lust-inducing brew. Roses (rose hips included) have long been associated with love and are thus an obvious choice for this kind of tea. And so is jasmine, another well-known love herb.

Herbs are used in a variety of ways in magic; for example, they can be infused into oils or alcohol, or they can be physically processed to extract the essential oils, as well as the aforementioned tisanes (teas made without leaves from the tea plant). Infusions don't have to be made hot to extract the essences needed from the herbs, cold infusions are just as useful and might even be better for a given need. Also, it just might not be possible to get some herbs to a high enough temperature, which is one of the advantages of cold infusions.

In general, hot infusions are superior for processing lactones, iridoids, and tannins. On the other hand, delicate oils, antioxidants, polysaccharides, nutrients, and specific kinds of teas are best handled using the cold infusion method. Don't worry; I will talk in more detail about both methods in the second part of this book.

Overall, remember that experimenting with different ingredients and merging them into one powerful and unique spell is probably the most exciting aspect of magic. Making magical teas, potions, and infusions are all excellent ways to start practicing tea witchcraft, no matter your experience level. You can do so by simply researching the magical characteristics of the different ingredients, preparing your unique mix, and then charging it for specific goals.

Base Teas and their Magical Properties

So, how exactly should you prepare your magical tea?

To start, you need loose leaf tea. You can use any of the four main teas as a base: black tea, white tea, green tea, or oolong tea. Since the tea base is generally considered the neutral component of the spell, you can choose it simply on the basis of flavor if you intend your tea for drinking. But, you can also pick a specific base considering its magical properties. In any case, once you've made your selection, you will also need to choose the other elements to combine with the base tea. This is the most enjoyable part. You'll see how fun it is investigating various dried fruits, plants, and flowers and discovering what kinds of magical and mundane properties they have!

But for now, let's focus on the magical and health benefits of the four teas you can use as your base, which are all made from leaves known as *Camellia Sinensis*. And if you want to choose by more than just taste preferences consider that they can be divided according to the year's season.

Black Tea

Of all the teas, black tea is the most oxidized and fermented. It has shriveled and black tea leaves, and it can help with digestive issues, heart problems, asthma, high cholesterol, and menstrual issues. It carries a significant amount of caffeine - 47 mg, which is still less than coffee- and drinking too much of it can cause stomach acidity.

Pu-erh, or post-fermented black tea, is a subtype of black tea. Because it is rare and precious, some people consider it the "purest" of all teas, connecting it to the aether.

Colors: Black and Red
Crystal: Obsidian
Element: Fire
Energy: Masculine
Planet: Mars
Season: Winter
Magical Correspondences:

- Banishing Boredom and Negativity
- Courage
- Mind Stimulation

- Money
- Stability
- Strength

Common Types of Black Tea

- Assam
- Ceylon
- Constant Comment
- Darjeeling
- Earl Grey
- English Breakfast
- Irish Breakfast
    - Keemun
    - Lapsang Souchong
    - Orange Pekoe

Green Tea

Green tea is not fermented, just lightly steamed before drying. It offers numerous health benefits, including detoxification, weight loss, increased immunity and stamina, and blood glucose control. It contains less caffeine than black tea, although you should know that it still has some.

Colors: Green and Orange
Crystal: Malachite
Element: Fire
Energy: Masculine
Planet: Mars
Season: Summer
Magical Correspondences:

- Cleansing
- Conscious Mind
- Energy
- Health
- Love
- Money
- Passion
- Progress

Common Types of Green Tea

- Bancha
- Dragonwell
- Genmaicha
- Gunpowder
- Gyokuro
- Houjicha
- Jasmine
- Matcha
- Pi Lo Chun tea
- Pouchong
- Sencha
- Twig Tea
- White Monkey Paw
- Young Hyson

Oolong Tea

Because it is partially fermented, Oolong tea is often described as in-between green and black. It can aid with weight loss and stress management, blood sugar control, free radical removal, and skin and bone health. However, since it sweeps out excess calcium, too much of this tea might hasten bone deterioration. Also, it contains a lot of caffeine.

Colors: Dark Blue and Purple
Crystal: Amethyst
Energy: Feminine
Element: Water
Planet: Mars and Moon
Season: Autumn
Magical Correspondences:

- Concentration
- Divination
- Emotional Balance
- Friendship
- Love
- Meditation
- Reflection
- Romance

- Serenity

Common Types of Oolong Tea

- Formosa
- Iron Goddess of Mercy
- Milk Oolong
- Phoenix Tea
- Wulong

White Tea

This is a little more difficult tea to come by. Its leaves have been harvested young and very lightly steamed, or not treated at all. Some include a trace of caffeine. White tea is a powerful antioxidant and antibacterial that benefits the health of the heart, mouth, and skin. Drinking two cups is generally better than one, and you may reuse the tea leaves, albeit the second cup will take longer to brew.

White teas come in various flavors and are typically classified by their flavors. You might have to look for some in a tea store.

Colors: Gold, White, and Yellow
Crystal: Quartz
Element: Fire and Air
Energy: Masculine
Planet: Sun and Mars
Season: Spring
Magical Correspondences:

- Aura Healing
- Clarifying
- Cleansing
- Connection with Deities and Spirits
- Fertility
- Happiness
- New Beginnings
- Psychic Abilities
- Purification
- Wisdom
- Youth

Common Types of White Tea:

- Long Life Eyebrow
- Silver Needle
- White Darjeeling
- White Peony
- Yin Zhen

If you need a tea base that is not actually from the tea plant, whether for taste or caffeine or any other reason, you can also use Yerba Mate or Rooibos as bases for your teas.

Herbal Tisanes & Infusions

As previously discussed, we also have herbal tisanes, made without any tea (camellia). In this case, magical qualities depend entirely on the utilized herbs. Being made up of dried, unprocessed herbs, seeds, fruits, or roots and generally having no caffeine (unless the herb does), this kind of beverage is generally quite popular among witches. Also, because herbals are simple to make, many recipes are available. Overall, herbal tisanes and infusions improve relaxation, lowers cholesterol, and decrease the risk of heart disease, cancer, and diabetes. However, they tend to have fewer antioxidants than actual teas because of the absence of real tea leaves.

Chamomile, Ginseng, Hibiscus, Peppermint, Rooibos, and Spearmint are all well-known examples of tisanes. However, herbal doesn't always mean soothing - Yerba Mate is an herbal infusion that contains a very high caffeine content, suppresses hunger, and can become addicting. So, use caution if you start drinking it regularly!

How to Make your Magic Tea

Even if you're new to tea witchcraft, I'm sure you already know there are several ways to prepare tea and various tools to do that. For most people, buying your tea base is easiest and then you can buy or grow the herbals, then strain them out using a tea ball or infuser before consuming.

And what if all you can afford is a carton of grocery store tea bags? Don't worry, leaving aside tasseography, that's perfectly fine as well. And, just as you would do with loose leaf tea, you can cut the tea bag open and utilize the herbs and leaves inside for something else. For example, you can make a dream pillow with chamomile. Alternatively, you can brew a magical bath tea by tossing the tea bags directly into your bath water. You can prepare a hot tea, let it cool, and then pour it into a spray bottle to use around the house to purify your property or to bring prosperity, serenity, and love.

If possible, choose organic or all-natural tea bags when buying pre-made teas. Even better, would be to get organic herbal infusions and loose-leaf herbs in bulk, which you can find online from a variety of retailers at a reasonable price. The best way to create EXTRA strong tea magic is to grow your own fruit, flowers and herbs.

Temperatures and Brewing Time

Every kind of tea has a preferred water temperature for brewing and a specific time range for steeping that allows for the best flavor. For example, white or green teas should be treated in the gentlest way possible and steeped at a lower temperature to maintain their delicate taste. On the other hand, black teas and rooibos can handle the heat of boiling water without damaging taste or beneficial elements. Unfortunately, since so many herbs can be brewed to make tea, it is impossible to provide an exact steeping and brewing guide for all of them.

Below you can find approximate temperatures and brewing times for the most common kinds of tea. Of course, you can adjust them depending on your personal taste and the flavor you want to get.

White Tea:
Temperature: 175-180 °F (79-82 °C)
Brewing Time: 4 minutes

Green Tea:
Temperature: 175-180 °F (79-82 °C)
Brewing Time: 3 minutes

Oolong Tea:
Temperature: 180-195 °F (82-90 °C)
Brewing Time: 3 minutes

Black Tea or Rooibos:
Temperature: 205-212 °F (96-100 °C)
Brewing Time: 5 minutes

Herbal Tisanes:
Temperature: 205-212 °F (96-100 °C)
Brewing Time: 5+ minutes

Tea Offerings for Deities and Ancestors

As briefly mentioned before, you can craft tea blends as offerings for deities, spirit guides, and ancestors. Even though you can offer them the tea you like the most, it would be advisable to get to know their preferences - green tea? Red clover tisane? Chamomile, maybe? You'll definitely have to experiment with different libations to determine what your guides prefer.

And why should you craft teas for the gods, goddesses, and other spirits? Well, building a connection with one's deity is an ongoing process, just like any other relationship. It's a never-ending work of giving and receiving. And making this kind of offering is a great way to express your gratitude and strengthen your bonds with them. Hoping that, in return, they will bless you. In fact, this is precisely why tea-making and brewing have been practiced for thousands of years and the reason why our ancestors used to offer tea to the gods. Today, we can follow their footsteps and make tea to honor the spiritual beings we want to call on.

First of all, find out about traditional tea offerings. Consider the culture from which your deity comes. Are we talking about a Danish Norse god? Are they an Irish Celtic deity? An Egyptian goddess from the Cleopatra era? See what traditional teas from that time and culture you may find online. Chamomile tea, for example, was popular among ancient Egyptians, making it an excellent gift for the Egyptian sun gods Ra and Horus, and the goddesses Bastet and Sekhmet. Also, try to think outside the box. What do I mean by that? Teas produced with red clover blossoms, dandelions, yarrow, nettles, and elderflower tend to be favorites of Celtic gods. Blackberry, pine, nettles, and dandelion are highly appreciated in the Norse pantheon. Lavender, dandelion, almonds, mugwort, and all herbs that appear to be linked with the goddess Hecate will quickly come up in a Google search. So, in this case, a tea with lavender and almonds might be a great option. How you ultimately determine which herbs and flowers are best for a particular diety for your practice might be as easy as an internet search or perusing books you already have. Or you can check with other neo-pagans in person or online chat groups for their suggestions.

And what if you can't discover any traditional teas associated with your deity? In this case, consider herbs that grow wild in the area where your god or goddess is from. For example, if your chosen goddess is Brigid, you could investigate the wild herbs that can be found throughout Ireland. Buttercup, clover, borage, daisy, and anjelica are some of the plants that may appear in the results. So, make a list, and then start researching the plant qualities - especially whether these plants are non-toxic and edible if you intend to drink the tea you are about to make for your deity.

After this research, you'll be finally ready to put everything together. Let's imagine you want to offer your god or goddess nettles, chamomile, and roses. You can combine the ingredients, cover it with hot water, and serve it to them as a tea gift. However, if you want to go all out, you can choose to turn your tea offering into a full-fledged ceremony, complete with incantation during the brewing process, moonlight charging, and altar placement. Your magic, your choice.

But... is it truly advisable for you to consume the tea as well? Drinking the same beverage you're offering to your deity can be really enlightening, in my opinion. It's almost as if you're having a tea party with them! However, you should keep your offering tea separate from your cup of the same brew. And, once finished, leave it outside for at least a few hours if you can, ideally all day or night. Then, pour it onto the ground.

Does this mean you should not drink the tea offer you made to your god or goddess? Well, my personal advice is indeed to avoid it. However, since we are talking about YOUR magic, you may also choose to sip the offering tea (only if the ingredients are safe for human consumption!). In this case, just inform your deity that the tea you are drinking was created in their honor and that you hope your sharing it makes it an appealing gift.

Once more, no matter the favorite herbs of your god or goddess, don't forget that you will always have to study and do your research before ingesting any! Many of them can be poisonous and have the potential to interact with other herbal supplements or medicines you might be taking. So, when in doubt, always consult a licensed health care professional.

Your Basic Tea Toolkit

No matter if you are going to prepare your magical tea for casting a spell or honoring a particular deity, you will need to use some specific tools. The following is a basic list to get you started. If you feel like your magic needs something else to be effective, just go ahead and follow your instincts. After all, when it comes to magic, YOU are in charge!

TEACUP AND SAUCER: you can choose the style you like the most. Just remember that for tasseomancy, a white or light-colored cup is the best option because it allows you to see the different symbols and figures quicker and more easily.

SPOON: any spoon will work, but, as we will see in a short while, a wooden one is considered the best option for this kind of magic.

TEA INFUSER: to make it easier to filter out your tea leaves and herbs, an infuser is a mini strainer to contain your tea/tisane ingredients while they steep.

MORTAR AND PESTLE: you can use them in case you need to grind up your herbs or spices.

STORAGE CONTAINERS: you will also have to decide which is the best place in your house to store your herbs and teas. You might opt for zip lock bags, glass vials, or mason jars. What really matters is that the container must be airtight and always kept in a cool and ideally dark place.

MAGICAL RECIPE BOOK: the enchanted place where you keep and store all the secrets of your magic. A simple notebook will work just fine, but you can also choose to buy a more elaborate (and generally more expensive) journal for witches. In any case, you will use your journal to document your spells and tea recipes - the combinations you like the most, those that didn't taste good to you or, those that didn't achieve the magical results you were hoping for.

How To Make Your Magic Tea Even More Powerful

Now that you know the basics of tea witchcraft, you can make your beverages even more magical and powerful. To do so, think of your preparation in the same way that you would do with a spell jar. Ask yourself questions such as: which herbs I am about to use and what kind of magical properties do they have? Do the ingredients I'm using correspond to my goals? Is this the proper tea for this occasion?

Remember that for any magical use, all plants can be "charged" for more potent magic. This allows you to combine your own energy with the herb's properties, amplifying the results.

To charge your tea or tisane ingredients, put the herb into a jar and gaze at it while maintaining a calm posture. This way, you will be able to feel the vibrations within the leaves, blossoms, and stems and see the energy emanating from the plants. Then, put your hand inside to touch the herbs to feel both your and the plant's strength mingling. Next, run your fingers through the herbs until you notice a tingling feeling from the energy they contain. When this happens, hold it still for a few seconds while envisioning your desire.

Now that the herbs are finally enchanted to help you through their magical properties, you can create a great variety of infusions tailored to your specific goals or feelings.

And, if you want to give it a little extra oomph, you can draw a symbol in the air above the kettle while you're waiting for the water to boil. A love rune, a health sigil, or even a word or number can help you with that. Recite your magical words over the tea while it steeps.

Once the tea is ready to drink, spend a few moments to properly set your intentions. If your tea magic is for healing, the exercise of forming a ball of healing energy in the palm of your hands can be quite beneficial. Then, allow that energy and intention to pervade your drink before consuming it or offering it to your favorite deity. Take a moment to truly enjoy what you've created, thoroughly absorbing the flavor and texture of your tea as you sip it. Remember that to advance something forward, you can stir the tea clockwise; to reverse it, you can stir it counter-clockwise. To add some extra energy to your purpose, stir your beverage three times clockwise with a dedicated wooden spoon.

While drinking your tea, feel it enter your body, and envision your intention filling and encircling you, changing your life path. Always focus on your motivation. If your spell is about making new friends, imagine this same wish as in a video: what are you doing with them? Are you chatting, laughing, or having dinner together? In other words, while drinking the tea, take the time to imagine your purpose coming true. Inhale your intention and, if you want, write a poem or a specific spell that expresses your desire and recite it aloud. Imagine your body acting as a magnet, drawing what you want into your life.

As mentioned before, remember that you can also choose to keep the leftovers of your tea and use them in other magical ways. For example, you can utilize them as a hair rinse, to feed your plants, in a ceremonial bath, and obviously, as we will see in greater detail soon, for tea leaf reading.

Quick & Easy Spells with Base Teas

For the sample spells below, use teabags to keep it easy. This way, you will see how you can carry out rituals for important purposes even with the quickest and cheapest option.

BLACK TEA SPELL FOR WEALTH: before putting a black tea bag in the water, hold it in your hands. While you do it, visualize money coming to you as you become increasingly wealthy. Spend some minutes visualizing your desire, then drink your tea as usual.

GREEN TEA SPELL FOR CLEANSING: before putting the green tea bag in the water, hold it in your hands. Imagine water going through your body, purifying it, and removing all the negative energies. Feel how it cleanses and detoxifies you. After a few moments of visualization, drink your tea as you would always do.

OOLONG TEA SPELL FOR LOVE: before putting the tea bag in the water, hold it in your hands. Imagine the person of your dreams and visualize love coming into your life. Concentrate on as many details as you can. Then, drink your tea.

WHITE TEA SPELL FOR ENERGY: before putting the tea bag in the water, hold it in your hands. Visualize the flow of magical energy through your body. Feel it coming from the tea bag all around you and within you. After a few moments of visualization, drink your tea.

Extra Magical Tips for your Teas

- If you want to defend yourself from negativity and provide extra strength and power to your potion, use black tea as your base.
- Use a special consecrated spoon to mix your magical potions (as previously mentioned, a wooden one is generally the best option).
- A particular teapot and a special teacup can also be consecrated (in both cases, you can use earthenware or ceramic.)
- Consider using two separate cups: one for divination and the other for other magical infusions.
- Always use the recipe that best corresponds to your desire or purpose to harness the maximum powers of the herbs.

I cannot stress this enough: **only use herbs you know for sure you're not allergic to, that are safe for human consumption, and that are safe to take in case of being pregnant or breastfeeding or any medical condition**. But once you know that you can use an herb safely, you can add two extra teaspoons of herbs per cup if you want to boost their effectiveness (and the flavor potenecy).

Special Tea Ceremony Spell

Now, I would like to briefly talk to you about a very special ceremony I learned about reading the book "A Victorian Grimoire" by Patricia Telesco.

I first read about it several years ago, but I still perform it to encourage sharing and open communication with my fellow tea-loving witches.

For the ceremony, you need:

- As many light pink tea lights or little candles as there are people in the room (you can substitute yellow or white if pink is not your favorite color).
- One large pillar candle in light pink (or white or yellow, according to the previously chosen color).
- One pot of tea (you can use hibiscus, earl grey with lemon, or lavender).

- Teacups, one per person. You can tie a silver ribbon for communication, or a violet one for enchantment, around the teacups' handles to increase the magical boost.

Once you have everything that you need, place the tea set on a tablecloth and make sure it includes everything you and the other witches will need to enjoy your tea (lemon slices, sugar, milk, etc.)

Place a small candle next to each cup but don't ignite it just yet. Instead, turn on whatever music you like while lighting the main candle. Light tea lights in turn after you and your guests have seated. Then, simply enjoy your time while sipping your tea. As each witch finishes and leaves, blow out the candles. Last but not least, blow out the pillar and bless the ritual with words of your choice.

Tea Meditation

Even if you don't feel the need to cast a particular spell, tea drinking has been a soothing and comforting ritual for many civilizations throughout history, and it is still practiced today. It helps you to relax, can focus your mind, or enable you to connect with people. And it can bring you a sense of stillness, gratitude, and peace, especially if carried out in an environment where you feel safe and at ease.

Being mindful and present throughout your entire tea ritual, from brewing the tea, drinking it, and observing the effects on your mind and body is a form of meditation – tea meditation. You can perform it at any time of day: in the morning to start your day with presence, in the middle of the day for enhancing attention and clarity, or in the evening for a peaceful night's sleep (just remember to use herbs such as chamomile or valerian instead of tea!)

Tea meditation offers many emotional and physical advantages. For example, it decreases anxiety and stress while boosting focus, gratitude, and a sense of calm. It helps to improve your mental health and can enable you to sleep and rest better.

Magical Correspondences

Let's now focus on the most important correspondences you will have to take into account when preparing your tea.

In witchcraft, correspondences are links between the intangible and the physical, something you can form with the tools you use to cast your spell, the time you choose to cast it, and much more.

For example, if you intend to cast a love spell, it is best to do it on a Friday, the day of Venus, using a pink candle, the color of love.

Overall, it takes a bit of intuition and creativity to combine all of the parts to create an effective spell. When specifically talking about tea magic, let's imagine for a moment that you wish to get a job that makes you happy and where you have the chance to work with nice and friendly colleagues. Well, in this case, you could choose amaranth, which represents stability, and yerba mate, which corresponds to happiness. Or, perhaps, you wish to make new friends with whom you can go out and have fun. If that's the case, you might brew a blend that includes licorice root and rose for lovely and healthy connections, as well as chamomile for luck. In short: there are so many ways to put the magical properties of the herbs together, how you do it is going to be unique to you.

I recommend you learn as much as you can about tea and tisane ingredients to better comprehend what attributes the different herbs contain so you can maximize their power in your magic.

Also, consider that environmental conditions and personal feelings might also influence an ingredient's common features and correspondences. Therefore, I also advise you conduct some tests to see how the different herbs affect YOU and YOUR magic.

Herbs for Magical Teas and their Correspondences

As you will read later, many herbs can be utilized to increase the enchantment power of your tea. Below is a basic list of some herbs, flowers, and spices you can add to a tea, along with their magical properties.

Once more, pay attention to the ingredients you use and be sure you're not allergic to them or otherwise unable to take them.

Please note: mugwort is listed below and in some of the book's recipes. **This flowering plant is sometimes considered poisonous**; however, the truth is that for years, natural health practitioners have employed mugwort in **tiny doses**. This plant can help you feel more energized, calm your stomach, and have minor psychoactive effects. However, in excessive amounts, it might be dangerous to some people. If you want to use it in your tea but are unsure about quantities, just buy a readymade mix containing a little mugwort and dose it according to the package guidelines. **If you are pregnant or allergic to the Asteraceae or Ragweed family, then avoid ingesting mugwort.**

On the other hand, **valerian** is a potent sedative with varying effects on different people. You might want to start with a tiny dose of this herb to see how it affects your body. Above all, **stop using ANY plant and visit a doctor if you experience any kind of adverse effects**.

Amaranth: protection, strength, stability, self-control, commitment

Basil: wealth, money, blessings, fertility, protection, house blessings

Bergamot: stop magical interference, protection from illness and evil

Cardamom: lust, love, keeping a partner faithful

Catnip: love, beauty, happiness, working with cat spirits

Chamomile: luck, sleep, healing, peace, purification, relaxation, calm, abundance

Cinnamon: creative projects, sexuality, lust, passion, consecration, love, psychic powers, independence, brilliance, community building

Cowslip (Primula veris): success in treasure hunting

Damiana: visions

Dandelion root: spirit work, divination, dream magic

Echinacea: strength, natural defenses

Elderberry: exorcism, healing, prosperity, protection

Eucalyptus: protection

Eyebright: mental and psychic powers

Forget-Me-Not: dream fulfilment, accepting emotions, artistic projects

Ginger: power, success, confidence, prosperity, sense of adventure, sensuality, protection

Ginseng: achievement of goals, protection, beauty, love

Hawthorn berries: psychic and extrasensory abilities

Hibiscus: divination, love, dream magic

Honeysuckle: quick abundance, prosperity

Jasmine: healing, wisdom, self-transformation, love

Lavender: anti-anxiety, sleep, healing, meditation, psychic abilities, dream fulfillment, truth

Lemon: removing energy blockages, cleansing

Lemongrass: psychic opening, cleansing

Licorice root: healthy relationships, harmony, friendship

Mugwort: astral projection, protection of travelers, lucid dreaming

Orange peel: luck, money, accomplishments, recognition, joy, charm

Peppermint: purification, love, anti-negativity, psychic and mental power, clarity

Primrose: protection, encounters

Rooibos: courage, strength, patience, determination

Rose: simplicity, love, affection, healing sexuality

Rose Hips: healing, good luck, love

Rosemary: cleansing, drawing the aid of spirits, mental focus

Valerian: relaxation, protection, curing insomnia

Willow: protection

Wintergreen: protection

Witch Hazel Bark (Hamamelis): protection

White Oak Bark (Quercus alba): protection, power, and luck

Wormwood: astral travels, spirit world, psychic dreaming

Other Magical Correspondences

But other correspondences can assist you in getting the absolute best out of your magical tea. For example, different ingredients on specific days of the week or Moon phases for different goals. When preparing your tea, you can choose whether you feel like the extra boost these items offer is appropriate, depending on your practice and beliefs, and taste preferences.

Common Tea Extras

Cream: fertility, creativity, health, abundance, happiness, employment
Honey: love, lust, sex, attraction, binding, health
Sugar: attraction, love, wisdom, sympathy

Moon Phases

How can you determine which Moon phase is the most suitable to perform or create a particular tea spell? Overall, drinking tea on a full Moon is always a safe bet and highly helpful for a variety of magical intentions. But each specific phase can boost specific purposes.

Phase 1: New Moon

The New Moon marks a new beginning. When the Moon is in this phase, it is barely visible or completely dark, and the sky is generally black. With the Moon hidden, you are better able to recognize your dark sides, the ones you usually prefer to keep secret.

For example, you might have a manipulative side that you normally say doesn't exist when someone says you are acting a certain way. Well, there are always healthy ways to use those particular abilities and the New Moon is the perfect time to make them work in a positive way.

Also, since New Moons mean new beginnings, this is a beautiful moment to set goals and intentions for the next cycle. Is there anything you want to see happening in the next 30 days? Is there a toxic lover you are finally ready to cut out of your life to make room for the person you have always dreamt of? Well, the New Moon is your chance to start anew, especially in love. So, if you feel ready to let go of the past and attract the right partner for you, this phase of the Moon offers you just such an opportunity.

The spells and rituals of this phase can be performed from the day of the New Moon until three days after it.

Examples of themes to work on in this phase:

- Any new project or task
- Love and relationships
- Goal setting and objectives
- Health, beauty, and self-care
- Job search
- New beginnings

Phase 2: Waxing Crescent Moon

The Waxing Crescent Moon phase takes place when the Moon starts to become visible in the sky, as it starts moving from a New Moon to a Full Moon. During this time, the Moon grows, becomes brighter, and creates an ideal space for sympathetic magic around growth. What is sympathetic magic? The one that works through symbolic similarity. The Moon is starting to glow again, so it's essential to use that energy to make your career, self-esteem, and love life shine brighter as well.

The spells and rituals of this phase can be performed three and a half to seven days after the New Moon.

Examples of themes to work on in this phase:

- Emotions
- Business and Work
- Changes and New Beginnings
- Projects and Ideas
- Preparation of Amulets and Other Magical Tools
- Animals

Phase 3: First Quarter

This is the phase in which we see half of the Moon. And as the days go by, the illuminated portion of the Moon grows larger and larger.

It is an excellent time to build and the best phase to lay the foundation for something solid and lasting. If there are aspects of your life that you cannot put in order or are not working as you would like them to, this Moon phase offers you a new opportunity.

The spells and rituals of this phase can be performed seven to ten days after the New Moon.

Examples of themes to work on in this phase:

- Health
- Good luck
- Motivation
- Friends and Personal Relationships
- Inner Strength and Courage
- Projects

Phase 4: Waxing Gibbous Moon

This phase occurs when the Moon is more than half full, and its illuminated surface continues to increase towards being a Full Moon. The word "gibbous" is of Latin origin and means "hump," a term used for centuries to indicate round shapes.

The Waxing Gibbous Moon phase is an excellent time to make important and much-needed changes. Don't panic if you have cast a spell that doesn't seem to have the desired effect. Sometimes a gestation period is necessary, and during this time, it might take time for the effect to be seen.

Relax and begin planning any other magical rituals you want to perform, taking advantage of the energy building toward the upcoming Full Moon.

The spells and rituals of this phase can be performed between ten and a half to fourteen days after the New Moon.

Examples of themes to work on in this phase:

- Love and Romance
- Dreams
- Creative projects
- Spirituality
- Patience
- Inspiration

Phase 5: Full Moon

With the Full Moon, emotions run high, and everything becomes much more intense. You can use its potency and apply it to basically any spell you want, knowing that you will count on all the Moon's power to help you. You can also charge your crystals during a Full Moon by placing them in a spot where they are directly exposed to lunar light. Another trick is to make Moon Water by leaving a cup of water under its light.

You can perform any magic under a Full Moon with extra power, keeping in mind that this is also a time when psychic abilities are intensified.

This phase's spells and rituals can be performed fourteen to seventeen and a half days after the New Moon.

Examples of themes to work on in this phase (although the Full Moon is excellent for virtually every type of magical ritual):

- Money and Work
- Love and Romance
- Dreams
- Family Relationships
- Fertility
- Protection

Phase 6: Waning Gibbous Moon

The waning gibbous phase is the period of time when the Moon darkens again, beginning the transition from a Full Moon to a New Moon. In general, it is the perfect moment to get rid of anything that keeps you negatively attached, for example, bad habits or addictions.

The Waning Gibbous Moon can help you cut ties with a past lover. It also marks an excellent time to rid yourself of negative feelings such as doubt and insecurity.

The spells and rituals of this phase can be performed three and a half to seven days after the Full Moon.

Examples of issues to work on in this phase:

- Stress
- Emotions
- Addictions of All Kinds
- Difficult Decisions
- Separations and Divorces
- Doubts and Insecurities

Phase 7: Last Quarter Moon

This lunar phase corresponds to the days when it is possible to see the Moon in the sky during the dawn and the morning, and it is characterized by the fact that exactly half of the Moon is illuminated after the Full Moon. For the northern hemisphere, the left side is shining, while for the southern hemisphere, it is the opposite.

The Last Quarter Moon is the ideal time to release any negativity that surrounds you and continue with any work of banishment that you previously started.

The spells and rituals of this phase can be performed seven to ten and a half days after the Full Moon.

Examples of themes to work on in this phase:

- Sleep
- Banishment
- Negativity
- Addictions of All Kinds
- Difficult Decisions
- Doubts and Insecurities

Phase 8: Waning Crescent Moon

This is the last visible phase of the lunar cycle, and this is when your attention should be focused on self-care and rest to replenish all possible energies for the next one.

It is also important to recognize your hopes and dreams and to cultivate your link with the divine and spiritual as much as possible.

Take advantage of the energy of this Moon to practice forgiveness and self-compassion to heal your inner wounds. This phase also favors the relaxation process and makes it possible to obtain important information from dreams and the unconscious.

As far as possible, you should adopt an attitude of relaxation and recollection, and avoid initiating new projects or undertaking new and risky actions.

Examples of themes to work on in this phase:

- Healing
- Relaxation
- Spirituality
- Self-care
- Forgiveness
- Cleansing

Special Moon: Black or Dark Moon

This phenomenon lasts approximately two to three days, during which the Moon is not visible in the sky at all.

This is also the perfect time to get rid of things in your life that you no longer want while at the same time contemplating all that you have already accomplished and what you want to achieve in the future.

In case you have to deal with any kind of enemy, it is advisable to start at this time.

This is also an excellent phase for taking care of yourself and finding comfort in seclusion.

The spells and rituals of this special phase can be performed keeping in mind that the black Moon occurs once every 32 months and that this phenomenon can last from one and a half to three and a half days.

Examples of themes to work on in this phase:

- Enemies

- Obstacles
- Achievements
- Things to eliminate
- Cleanliness
- Self-care

The Days of the Week

Among the different things to consider when preparing your magical tea is the day of the week on which it will be brewed. Each day of the week has a connection with a particular planet and is associated with masculine or feminine energy, a god or a goddess, earth elements, stones and crystals, and so on.

When casting a spell, it is advisable to look for the magical day of the week with the attributes that can best favor your efforts in tea witchcraft.

That said, keep in mind that the day of the week does not have the same importance as the phase of the Moon. If you are able to coordinate the right day with the most auspicious lunar phase, you will prepare an even more powerful tea and further increase your chances of success.

However, if everything else is perfect, don't delay preparing your magical tea because the day of the week doesn't seem to be the most appropriate. Your magic has a higher purpose that will make the day you cast your spell being perfect for YOU. With this in mind, let's look at the main magical correspondences of the seven days of the week:

SUNDAY

Name Origin: Sun
Planet: Sun
Energy: Male
Deities: Brigid, Ra, Apollo, and Helios
Colors: Gold, Yellow
Crystals: Topaz, Sunstone, Amber, Quartz, Diamond, Carnelian, Tiger Eye
Herbs: Marigold, Sunflower, Cinnamon, St. John's Wort, Incense
Associations: Success, Prosperity, Fame, Strength, Wealth, Promotion, Miracles, Healing

MONDAY

Name Origin: Moon
Planet: Moon
Energy: Feminine
Deities: Moon, Artemis, Diana, Selena, Thoth
Colors: White, Silver, Pearl, Light Blue, Light Gray
Crystals: Moonstone, Opal, Aquamarine, Pearl, Selenite
Herbs: Willow, Lotus, Chamomile, Catnip, Peppermint, Sage, Comfrey
Associations: Intuition, Fertility, Dream, Dreaming, Illusion, Femininity, Peace, Spirituality, Justice

TUESDAY

Name Origin: Germanic & Norse God Tyr
Planet: Mars
Energy: Masculine
Deities: Tyr, Mars, Morrighan, Tiwaz, Lilith, Aries
Colors: Red, Pink, Orange, Black
Crystals: Bloodstone, Rhodonite Flint, Garnet, Ruby, Rhodonite
Herbs: Holly, Basil, Cactus, Thistles
Associations: War, Courage, Rebellion, Protection, Conflict, Success, Strength

WEDNESDAY

Name Origin: Norse God Odin (Germanic God Woden)
Planet: Mercury
Energy: Masculine
Deities: Woden, Mercury, Hermes, Athena Lady Fortuna, Odin, Lugh
Colors: Yellow, Magenta, Orange, Purple
Crystals: Agate, Citrine, Aventurine
Herbs: Lilies, Lavender, Eucalyptus, Fern, Aspen, Aspen
Associations: Business, Arts, Chance, Transportation, Wisdom, Healing, Communication, Creativity, Fortune, Debt, Contracts, Music, Education

THURSDAY

Name Origin: Norse God Thor
Planet: Jupiter
Energy: Masculine
Deities: Thor, Zeus, Jupiter, Juno
Colors: Royal Blue, Green, Purple
Crystals: Lapis Lazuli, Lepidolite, Sugilite, Amethyst, Turquoise
Herbs: Oak, Clove, Sage, Honeysuckle, Lemon Balm
Associations: Honor, Wealth, Abundance, Loyalty, Business, Travel, Education, Healing, Harvest, Prosperity

FRIDAY

Name Origin: Germanic Goddess Frigga, Norse Goddess Freya
Planet: Venus
Energy: Feminine
Deities: Freya, Venus, Aphrodite
Colors: Pink, Gray, White, Water
Crystals: Jade, Lapis Lazuli, Coral, Malachite, Coral, Rose Quartz, Emerald
Herbs: Feverfew, Cardamom, Saffron, Apple Blossom, Strawberry
Associations: Love, Romance, Friendship, Covenants, Grace, Balance, Prosperity, Passion, Fertility, Birth, Pregnancy

SATURDAY

Name Origin: Roman God Saturn
Planet: Saturn
Energy: Masculine
Deities: Hecate, Saturn
Colors: Black, Grey, Red, Dark Purple
Crystals: Obsidian, Jet, Serpentine, Hematite, Apache Teardrop
Herbs: Cypress, Black Poppy Seeds, Mullein, Thyme
Associations: Wisdom, Banishment, Psychic Attack, Self-Discipline

Candle Magic

As you probably already know, candles are a staple in most magical toolkits. They amplify and release energy, can be left (unlit, of course!) around the house to promote positive vibes, and are the perfect complement for tea spells.

In witchcraft, candles have long played an essential role as powerful and versatile magical tools. In spells and rituals, they can be used alone or in conjunction with other instruments and ingredients. And, whether used for magical purposes or in everyday life, candles emit beneficial, calming, and soothing energies.

Candles are most commonly used to represent colors. Each color has its own magical properties and spiritual meanings. If your spell requires a candle, but you don't have one of the exact color, you can substitute it with a natural beeswax candle or a white one and incorporate the required color in a different way. You can also spice up your candle with an essential oil that has the properties of the color in question.

You can boost the power of your tea rituals by drinking your tea in the light of one or more candles, whose color should match the aim of your brew.

Candle correspondences include, but are not limited to:

· **White**: promotes serenity and peace, enhances personal strength and insight

· **Black**: psychic protection

· **Green**: bringing your ideas to life, amplifying prosperity

· **Blue**: connect with your chakras, heal emotional wounds

· **Yellow**: boosts social skills, attracts new career opportunities

· **Red**: love, sex, passion

· **Pink**: romantic love, self-love

· **Purple**: spiritual enlightenment, creativity

· **Orange**: ambitions, courage, broaden horizons

· **Brown**: increasing resources, such as health, energy, possessions

· **Gold**: attracts money, business opportunities, prosperity

When casting a spell, always use a new candle. Otherwise, you run the risk of clouding the new magic with the intentions of your previous spell work.

The Best Tea for Every Zodiac Sign

Besides more general correspondences, you should also consider astrology-based tea properties. Yes, as you have probably already guessed, there are specific sign teas, and you can choose which is the most recommended herbal drink according to your zodiac sign. You can take into account astrology, but never shy away from exploring the magical properties of alternative tea blends.

Aquarius (January 21–February 19): Hibiscus Tea

The Aquarius witch is the most creative of all. Floral mixes like hibiscus tea can boost their creativity and imagination like nothing else. A tea created from flora is inherently appealing to a free-spirited Aquarius.

Pisces (February 20–March 20): White Tea

Witches born under the sign of Pisces are highly sensitive beings who experience a wide range of emotions on a daily basis. White tea blends are perfect for them due to their delicate flavor and gentle vanilla overtones.

Aries (March 21–April 20): Matcha Tea

Matcha tea is ideal for those who are enthusiastic, determined, and confident enough to always take a leap of faith. Daring Aries witches are drawn to energizing tea experiences because of the high caffeine content and various health advantages of strong tea brews.

Taurus (April 21–May 21): Rooibos Tea

Taurus witches are graceful in their movements and exemplify consistency. This is why rooibos tea is considered the ideal companion for them. The nutty and earthy flavor of rooibos is a fantastic match for the Taurus' humble character.

Gemini (May 22–June 21): Fruit Tea

These witches are generally the most inquisitive, constantly eager to try something new and fascinating. This is why fruit teas are ideal for them. A few examples include caramel peach, apple oolong, apple cinnamon, or strawberry.

Cancer (June 22–July 22): Chamomile

Cancer witches look for peace and tranquility above everything else. They are often insecure about the idea of leaving their comfort zone and prefer to enjoy the familiar. Chamomile, with its delicate flavor and calming properties, is perfectly suited for them.

Leo (June 23–August 21): Masala Chai

Leo witches are constantly on the lookout for the dynamic and the wild, and they are ready to take over whatever situation and space they enter. The equally unique Masala chai, whose brews are packed with unusual and exotic spices, is right what they need to enhance their already captivating personality.

Virgo (August 22–September 23): Black Tea

In whatever they undertake, the Virgos take a methodical approach. Even when it comes to magic, they are selective, logical, and practical in their approach. Black tea, which is filled with health benefits and available almost everywhere, is an excellent choice for Virgo witches who always want to get right to the point.

Libra (September 23–October 24): Mint Tea

For the Libra witch, maintaining balance is truly a way of life. They are endearing, magnetically drawn to beauty, and natural peacemakers. Mint tea has the same flavor profile: not too bitter, not too sweet; just the right amount of everything to please the senses.

Scorpio (October 24–November 22): Ginger Tea

"Intense" is the adjective that best describes the Scorpio witch, someone generally serious who keeps their eyes on their goals, with no room for distractions. These mysterious, independent souls are an excellent fit for the robust ginger tea flavor.

Sagittarius (November 23–December 22): Sencha Tea

Sagittarius witches represent the sun's brilliant rays. They enjoy connecting with the sun's warmth because they are optimistic and good-natured. Sencha tea is a renowned Japanese tea that is cultivated in the sun, making it the perfect beverage for a Sagittarius to enjoy.

Capricorn (December 23–January 20): Black Tea

Capricorn witches are like ambitious, wise owls. Dark teas like earl grey are ideal for helping them get their day started and facing all sorts of obstacles life might put in their way.

Tasseography

Now that you know a bit more about tea witchcraft in general, I would like to offer you, as promised, a bit more information on the reading of tea leaves.

The technique of finding symbols and interpreting messages discovered in the forms and combinations of tea leaves is known as tasseography or tasseomancy. Though the procedure is pretty simple, the results can be truly impressive, and this is why this magical art has been attracting witches for generations. However, tasseography still isn't as well-known as crystal magic or tarot reading, thus, it's also less well understood.

Anyhow, don't worry: tasseography, a strong and creative technique of exercising your intuition, is actually quite simple to learn. And it's a terrific alternative for anyone who wants to practice a unique form of divination using what can be easily found at home instead of having to buy several different (and sometimes expensive) tools.

So, how exactly does tasseography work? Well, tea leaf reading, like all divination methods, is founded on the idea of directing energy. When our magical intention is directed at the tea, the leaves become energy conduits that can mirror our past and future experiences. The leaves expose hidden obstacles, offer wisdom, and even present possible future paths when asked a question. The color, shape, density, and positioning of the hydrated tea leaves contain these magical messages.

And how should you get started? First of all, as you probably already imagine, you have to prepare a cup of tea.

Assemble your teacup (ideally, you should use a white or light-colored one to examine the leaf arrangements better), hot water, and tea leaves. Take into account that, in this case, tea bag contents will not function since the leaves are too finely cut and way too tiny to form discernible shapes. Tasseography requires loose leaf tea to work.

This is why you should begin with loose black tea or oolong tea leaves. Earl Grey tea and Darjeeling tea are considered two of the best varieties and are easy to find online or in grocery shops. Overall, loose leaves are ideal for accumulating silt, and, as a result, they tend to form patterns.

Green tea or herbal teas can also be used; however, tea with flower buds and petals should be avoided. The reason for this is that tea reading is most effective when the leaves are uniform in size. When dried flower buds or fruit peels are present in the tea, their size varies. This can cause problems with your reading and should be avoided...at least at first.

So, place your chosen tea leaves directly into the cup and pour the boiling water over them. You won't have to worry about straining with tasseography because the leaves will stay in the cup. At this point, take a few seconds to ponder your intentions as the tea steeps, then start passing your energy to the tea leaves.

When starting asking questions, remember that specificity is crucial, so make sure you only ask clear and simple questions and take into account that a broad query will elicit a general response. When the tea is at the correct temperature, you should start sipping it while thinking about what you're about to ask. You can begin the swirling-and-turning process when there is about a tablespoon of liquid left in the cup. This process means holding the cup in your left hand and swirling it from left to the right (clockwise) three times.

Next, invert the cup over a saucer gently and carefully, always with your left hand. Let the cup rest upside down for about a minute before rotating it three times. Then, return the cup to its upright position, with the handle pointing south. The tea leaves, embedded with knowledge and answers, should appear glued to the cup in a variety of shapes and clusters, ready to give you an answer to your question.

And how should you read their messages? The process of interpretation may appear intimidating at first, but don't worry. Tasseographers have noticed many common patterns and arrangements across history.

Symbols can mainly be divided into five categories: animals, objects, mythical beings, letters, and numbers. Their shapes might be easily visible at times. For example, a bird's wings can represent a successful journey or freedom. A cross, on the other hand, could indicate a roadblock or impending problems. It's important to note that not every formation requires interpretation; instead, you will have to concentrate on the symbols that are relevant to your own query.

The different parts of the cup have a specific meaning too. The handle, for example, has a significant purpose: it acts as an energy conduit, connecting the abstract and physical realms. It also represents you, the querent, and should face south to symbolize your current surroundings. The tea leaves that are close to the handle represent occurrences in your immediate environment; on the other hand, leaves directly across the handle (facing north) indicate exterior influences and difficulties.

Also, for divination, you should consider the cup as divided into three sections. The teacup's rim symbolizes the present, the sides indicate the near future, and the bottom represents the distant future. These parts can be used to determine timing (when is a particular situation more likely to occur?), connection (how distant are two individuals?), or intensity (will a specific situation be life-changing?), always depending on the question.

Before proceeding with some practical examples, I would like to offer you some suggestions to improve your reading technique.

So, before starting with the process:

- Try to rid your mind of any unwanted thoughts.
- Accept that you have to trust your gut and avoid second-guessing yourself.
- Take all the time you need and let things happen naturally.
- Examine the tea leaves' shapes and distribution calmly.
- Never try to force a response. Examine the tea leaves carefully and allow the answer to come to you.
- Allow some ambiguity. Tea leaf reading gives you clues, but the significance of the signs will change depending on the environment, context, and your own personal situation.

And now, let's analyze a few practical examples.

Imagine, for example, you are curious about when you'll meet your next romantic partner. Since the reading will obviously be centered on timing, it will be critical to consider all the three sections of the cup. So focus on whether the majority of the leaves are placed. For example, are they on the left side? Or at the bottom? You might identify a wavy line at the bottom left of your cup, indicating some sort of connection to the sea. This suggests that although you may not find love right away, your next companion could be someone from another country. You should also consider exploring your inner world before looking outward for love because water also represents emotions and psychics. Feeling strong and at ease with yourself will surely help you meet someone right for you.

Let's now imagine you are trying to figure out whether you should talk to your boss about a difficult situation at work. There's been a lot of tension with your colleagues lately, and you're not sure whether you should address it or let it go. So, let's pretend you see in your cup an obvious line of dots. In this case, you should take note of which chart zones they're connecting. Since your comfort zone is tied to these external conditions, this concern is clearly beginning to affect all aspects of your life. And this kind of line might also symbolize a chain. This means you're inextricably linked to your boss, whether you like it or not, and there is no way to avoid it. So, given these circumstances, it would be preferable to face the problem head-on. And you will indeed feel better and lighter once the situation has been discussed.

Then there's the context application. Let's say you come upon an "N" letter beside the symbol of a serpent. The serpent signifies danger or poor fortune. So, the presence of the letter "N" near this sign could indicate that you are in danger from someone whose name begins with "N."

In contrast, if the letter "N" appears near the symbol of a bird flying away from the cup's handle, this would most likely mean you are about to receive news from someone whose name starts with "N."

Tasseography Main Symbols

The truth is, I could fill this entire book with examples and still never come up with exactly what you see in your cup. So, the best way for you to get started is to just start reading. The following are some of the main symbols of tea leaf reading:

Acorn: continued and improved health.

Aircraft: symbol of a failed project. Aircraft can be planes, balloons, or anything similar.

Angel: good news, especially concerning love.

Apples: success in business or studies, long life.

Arrows: bad messages coming from the direction the arrow is pointing.

Ax: overcoming problems.

Anchor: success in love or business.

Birds: another image of good fortune. When flying, a piece of good news is coming; when resting, you will soon undertake a lucky journey.

Boat: the upcoming visit of a good friend.

Bouquet: an overall favorable circumstance.

Bridge: a positive and lucky journey.

Butterfly: pleasure and success.

Candle: symbol of enlightenment.

Car: wealth and happiness approaching.

Castle: unexpected monetary or general fortune.

Circles: presents or money.

Clouds: troubles, but when surrounded by dots they represent monetary success.

Clover: happiness, prosperity, and good luck.

Coffin: the death of a loved one, or lengthy sickness.

Compasses: business travels.

Cow: abundance and prosperity.

Crescent moon: fame and abundance. When cloudy, you will overcome any kind of problem.

Cross: death, delay, or troubles in general.

Crown: honor and success.

Dagger: help coming from friends.

Dragon: upcoming big changes.

Eagle: a change in housing that will lead to wealth and honor.

Elephant: happiness, health, and good luck.

Fish: upcoming positive news from a foreign country.

Fox: backstabbing from a dear friend.

Goat: your enemy.

Greyhound: hard work that pays off with a great fortune.

Gun: slander, disharmony.

Hammer: overcoming challenges in life.

Hat: success in life.

Heart: a lover. When it appears close to a ring, a marriage might be in the near future. When blurred, your lover shouldn't be trusted completely.

Heavenly Bodies (Star, Sun, Moon): good luck, success, and happiness.

Horseshoe: a lucky journey or success in choosing your partner.

Hourglass: imminent danger.

House: business success.

Kettle: death.

Kite: a long journey that will lead you to pride and self-esteem.

Knife: hatred and fighting.

Ladder: travels.

Letter: a letter that might be sent through the post means news. If there is an initial nearby, it is the bearer of the news. Dots with a letter means money, but if the image of the dots is cloudy, it means a loss of money.

Lines: a journey, travels or a voyage and, together with other symbols, its possible directions. Wavy lines represent difficult journeys. Straight lines generally symbolize happiness, peace, and long life. A long line represents a long journey. If the line gets to the cup's handle, this could indicate you should return home.

Mountain: it can represent a powerful friend, but if several mountains appear, powerful enemies.

Mushroom: a fight that ends up in the sudden separation of two lovers.

Owl: poverty or sickness.

Palm Tree: a good omen, success, marriage.

Pear: social status, wealth, and a possible financially beneficial move.

People: an overall positive symbol.

Pig: it can symbolize both jealous friends and a faithful lover.

Pine tree: serenity, happiness.

Rabbit: being successful in the city.

Rat: loss by the hand of employees or enemies.

Reptiles: arguments.

Ring: marriage. If the ring is at the cup's bottom, the marriage will never take place; if clouds surround it, it means this will be an unhappy union. And if a letter appears nearby, that's the initial of the future spouse.

Saw: strangers causing problems.

Scales: a lawsuit.

Scissors: a break-up, arguments, illness.

Shark: symbol of death or danger.

Sheep: success and abundance.

Ship: a happy journey.

Snakes: a bad omen, danger or poor fortune.

Squares: peace and serenity.

Star: good luck. When surrounded by dots, it also means honor and wealth.

Swan: happy love life, good luck in general.

Sword: lovers arguing. A broken sword signifies the upcoming win of an enemy.

Trees: prosperity, serenity, good luck. When surrounded by dots, it means fortune is to be found in the country.

Triangles: unexpected good luck.

Umbrella: annoyance and difficulties.

Unicorn: a scandal.

Wheel: an inheritance.

Worms: secret enemies.

Best Tips for Reading Tea Leaves

As I'm sure you're starting to understand, tasseography is quite a vast field. And even though there are no quick fixes for learning it, there are some pointers that can help you get reading.

- Start with the biggest signs and work your way down to the smallest ones when making forecasts. This assists you in predicting the events that are most likely to occur soon.

- Remember that a big number of forms indicates that you find yourself at a crossroads in life.

- Focus on whether the shapes are evenly distributed across the cup or concentrated in a few spots. This could assist in determining whether the events are dynamic or focused on a specific event or period.

- Don't rush through your readings; instead, look at the leaves, put the cup down, close your eyes, and then pick it up again. Repeat the process all the times you need. This can be beneficial in terms of allowing the mind to concentrate, process the information, and understand the hidden meaning of the leaves.

- Always maintain objectivity, examine various points of view, and be considerate.

- Keep a journal to help you improve your skills over time. When writing them down, be as specific as possible: it can help you with future readings.

As usual, when talking about magic, don't forget that neither the leaves nor the cup have any inherent power: the answers you read are, at the end of the day, a mirror of your own intuition. And once again, it takes time to develop divination skills. But the more you practice, the better you will get at reading responses. All the wisdom you'll ever need is already within you, so allow yourself to trust your instincts, and you will soon be able to master this magical ability.

Tea and the Magic of Color Healing

Did you know that tea's color, like that of any other food or drink, has a profound physical and psychological impact on the human body? Color has long been acknowledged for its healing properties, and Native American, Celtic, Central Asian, Middle Eastern, Chinese, Druidic, Greek, and Teutonic cultures all employed it. At Karnack and Thebes, ancient Egyptians even built color halls where they studied color therapy and performed color healing techniques.

Color psychology and color therapy are becoming increasingly important these days. Color healers, in fact, believe that disease is the result of an imbalance at one or more levels of the physical and spiritual bodies. These bodies are said to be linked to chakras, which, as you might already know, are energy centers in the human body.

Normally, each chakra absorbs light and filters the colors required to feed the body. But when one or more chakras are prevented from doing that and unable to process the ideal color frequencies, this results in an energy blockage. Consequently, the system is disrupted, which can lead your body to experience different kinds of diseases. Color can be used to restore balance in these affected areas.

When it comes to tea colors, there are a lot of things to consider. Altitude, climate, soil, weather conditions, where, when, how, and by who the tea was processed - all of these factors influence the color of a tea.

For example, tea that has been oxidized very little is greener, whereas tea that has been extensively oxidized is redder. Anyhow, every tea or herbal tisane will be colored in some way.

White (which commonly morphs into yellow), green, orange, red, and brown are the five fundamental tea colors. And then we also have black tea, the result of a strong brewing. Overall, white teas are calming and can be consumed for spiritual purposes, such as to improve meditation. Green is the color of harmony in the body, mind, and spirit and is also used to help one's health. Just consider that green tea does not always seem green in the cup - it could actually look yellow! Black teas, which can look dark red or orangey amber when brewed, generally boost energy. Brown-hued teas can aid with indecisiveness, concentration, and digestive system awakening.

Now, let's have a closer look at the specific characteristics of these teas.

Color Healing: White Tea

As you will have probably noticed, in the cup, most white tea leaves make the resulting tea liquid look yellow or transparent. The yellow color is a happy medium between the red and blue spectrums. Yellow is associated with creativity, generosity, inspiration, charisma, mental agility, and communication. When you wish to make a drastic change in your life, succeed in medicine, diplomacy, the performing arts, or counseling, or when your goal is to charm or persuade someone, then choose to drink yellow-colored teas.

These teas can also help you change your mindset. For example, you can break a bad habit, learn to accept a circumstance you can't change, or gain confidence to achieve your highest aspirations.

But white teas might also appear almost whitish after steeping, therefore they fall within the white group too in color healing. Clarity, spiritual enlightenment, clairvoyance, cleaning, healing, and truth searching are all represented by this color. White teas are beneficial for cleansing in terms of physical health.

Color Healing: Black Tea

Since some black tea leaves appear mahogany red in the cup after steeping, they are often linked to this color in color therapy. Red is associated with war, love, vitality, vigor, strength, willpower, courage, intensity, passion, and masculinity. So, drink red-colored teas to enhance your immune system after an illness and to alleviate the psychological impacts of the very same disease. A few herbal teas, such as rooibos, honeybush, hibiscus, and rosehips, look red too.

In the cup, other black tea leaves brew up orange. And teas with an orange hue help to clarify and invigorate the mind, and they're also known for being vision enhancers. They can help improve self-control, recharge left-brain batteries, and boost willpower and adaptability. They also assist a person in decluttering and organizing their mental closet. Last but not least, orange-looking teas may even inspire you to succeed and achieve your dreams.

Color Healing: Green Tea

Some green tea leaves do look green when brewed up; therefore, they are related to this color in color healing. Green is the most recurrent color in nature, and it perfectly sits between the red and blue extremes of the color spectrum. Nature has blessed us with an impressive amount of nutritious, emerald-colored teas: sencha, gyokuro, and matcha, as well as peppermint and spearmint herbal teas, are among them.

Overall, green is the color of wealth, good fortune, abundance, success, and renewal. Green teas can be taken to heal the spirit and create a happy home since green denotes peace, serenity, and harmony. They can also help restore balance in out-of-whack systems in the body.

Final Tips for Successful Magic

Before we get to the collection of tea recipes, and now that you know the main characteristics of tea witchcraft, I would like to offer you a few suggestions about magic in general.

I think this is important because when they start practicing spells, some people quickly become frustrated if they don't get the results they want or think they can get substantial changes in their lives in just a few days.

So, I want to share some fundamental considerations that are too often overlooked by those who begin this practice. Following these easy suggestions can help you to achieve real and lasting results, and hopefully you will not be disappointed if your wishes are not fulfilled as quickly as you would like.

First, magic does not guarantee specific results. Instead, it increases the likelihood that what you want will happen. Therefore, if you cast a spell to get something that has a zero percent chance of happening, no magic will make things change.

However, suppose you have interviewed for a job position that you are objectively qualified for. In that case, a success spell will increase your chances of being chosen among the various candidates.

As for practically everything in this life, in the case of witchcraft, too, practice makes perfect. If at first you fail to get satisfactory results with your magic, don't stop trying. It takes time, practice, and effort to improve your magical skills. You likely didn't walk the first time you tried it when you were a baby, so don’t expect magic to work right away either. You need to give yourself some time before you decide that a spell or ritual it's not right for you.

When casting a spell, you must be clear about your intentions and concentrate on the desired result. If you do it imprecisely, you will never achieve your goal. Don't be surprised if you make a new friend after a love spell. It possibly happened because you forgot to specify that what you wanted was romantic love, not a platonic one.

Also, remember that magic is not the same for everyone. What do I mean by that? There are, of course, general techniques for spell work, but it is essential to experiment, adapting every ritual to YOU and your needs.

Trial and error will be the way to figure out what works best for you. Remember that your magic combines external energies with your own internal energies, for a totally unique combination. In other words, no two witches’ spells or magic in this world will ever be exactly alike.

In the Universe, there are balances for everything, including magic. And in a spell, there must be reciprocity because there is an exchange of energies. As such, you cannot simply ask for or conjure a magical outcome without giving something in return. Some spells require an offering to the goddess or god. As we have seen, a cup of tea, for example. You can also try to reciprocate the help that is offered to you through simple acts of kindness, such as sharing your lunch with a co-worker who forgot theirs or holding a door open for someone.

If you use tools, you should try to choose those that are made of natural materials rather than artificial ones, such as a wooden spoon instead of a plastic one. Objects made from natural materials have inherent energies and the ability to hold and transfer them. In addition, this is better for the environment. For example, if left outdoors, a plastic wand or spoon will not decay for thousands of years, while a wooden one will do it in one or two.

If you're missing an ingredient, it is completely acceptable to use a substitute instead of forgoing your spell. For example, if an herb isn't available in your area and a similar one is, switching it up might increase the success of your magic rather than hinder it.

Once again, never use an ingredient or tool if you have an intolerance or allergy to that item or material. Instead, consult a list of correspondences and find an alternative - substituting one ingredient or tool for another does not mean that your magic will be less effective or that the result will be different. Just consider that, in the case of tea spells, the taste might change a bit.

Generally, a spell will be effective within a full lunar cycle. This is because it takes a bit of time for the magical energies to build up and be released. Also, it takes a LOT of energy to maintain your magical results over time. Therefore, longer-acting magic, such as abundance, binding, or protection spells, will need to be refreshed regularly, either monthly, bi-annually, or annually.

In magic, less is often more. Therefore, it is best to use a spell with enough power to give you the desired result but not go beyond that, as this could backfire on you.

It is crucial to think carefully about your desired magical results to determine which spell is best for you. For example, if you move to a new city and cast a generic friends attraction spell, this will spread far and wide, attracting anyone you might potentially want to start a conversation with.

That's great if you're looking to meet as many people as possible, but not so good if, for example, you're only interested in developing a small circle of friends with similar interests.

Also, if you choose to use words to accompany your spell, they should be your own if possible. This is because they will have more power coming from you than anyone who may have written them. However, if a spell is already worded in a way you feel comfortable with, there is nothing wrong with using those same sentences.

At the same time, while it is true that many magical chants often rhyme, rhyming is not mandatory when casting a spell. When writing a spell, your intention, your thoughts, and the words themselves are far more important than the specific way you express them.

A spell doesn't have to be particularly complex or elaborate to give you your desired magical results. In fact, as we have just seen, an effective spell can be the preparation of a simple cup of tea.

Also, magic should not be used to alter another person's free will, especially in a negative way. Doing so is rarely successful, and it is considered unethical except in a very narrow range of circumstances. For example, many witches would consider it acceptable to cast a spell to prevent someone from harming themselves or others.

Remember that spells can be difficult to break once cast, as the events have already been set in motion. Therefore, it is essential to be absolutely sure that you really need or want to cast a spell rather than trying to undo it afterward - better safe than sorry!

PART II

MAGICAL TEA RECIPES

Before discovering specific recipes for your magical teas and their methods of preparation, I would like to offer you a quick recap of some of the main goals you can achieve and desires you can express through specific herbs and plants. This way you will be able to quickly find ingredients that might assist in your purpose.

However, please remember this is a basic list and, as you will see in the recipes below, many more herbs exist, and the unlimited combinations of specific ingredients can offer other amazing results. Don't forget to experiment to find the herbs and blends that feel right for YOU and YOUR magic.

Herbs Recap

Magic for Money, Prosperity, and Luck

- Basil
- Chamomile
- Cinnamon
- Rosemary
- Spearmint

Magic for Good Sleep

- Chamomile
- Jasmine
- Lavander
- Lemon Balm
- Passion Flower
- Skullcup
- Valerian

Magic for Astral Travels and Psychic Dreams

These magical tisanes should be drunk before sleeping to produce psychic dreams.

- Chamomile
- Damiana
- Mugwort

- Peppermint
- Rose
- Rosemary
- Wormwood

Magic for Love

- Cherry
- Cinnamon apple
- Jasmine
- Lavender
- Red hibiscus
- Rosebud and rosehip
- Rosemary
- Strawberry

Magic for Long-Life and Vitality

- Ginseng
- Lemon
- Magnolia Bud
- Pau d' arco
- Peppermint
- Uva ursi

Magic to Cleanse the Aura

- Blue lotus
- Jasmine
- Peppermint
- Pomegranate
- Rosemary
- Sage
- Spearmint
- Tie Guan Yin

Magic for Divination

- Jasmine
- Mint
- Mugwort
- Mulberry
- Rose

Magic for Protection

- Burdock Root
- Juniper
- Lemon
- Rosemary

Magic to Enhance Your Beauty

- Hibiscus
- Lavender
- Lemon
- Pomegranate
- Rose

Magic for Emergency Spells

Warning: if you constantly cast emergency, speedy spells, the cosmos might end up not responding. After all, witchcraft should be something to perform regularly, not only when you need something. However, one day, every witch will require an "in case of emergency" spell, and some herbs are known to hasten the process. Just remember to be grateful when your wish comes true!

- Cayenne Pepper
- Cinnamon
- Ginger
- Yerba Mate

Practical Information about Methods of Preparation

Let's now briefly discuss how you can prepare your magical teas and infusions at home.

Basically, you can make teas by decoction or infusion, depending on the specific plants' parts you choose to use and the exact constituents you want to extract.

Infusions

An infusion is a form of maceration, and, in this case, water is poured over herbs to extract the active ingredients. The most common proportion, in general, and in the recipes we're about to see, is **1 to 2 tablespoons of herb to 1.5 cups of water**, though this may vary according to how strong you want your tea.

Aerial plant parts such as leaves, flowers, and soft berries are commonly used in infusions since hot water takes less time to extract the necessary ingredients. But watch out: if you boil the delicate leaves and blooms, you risk losing some of their strength due to evaporation and excessive heat. You can use barks and stems in infusions, but you will extract less of the essential oils and energies because water is usually not strong enough.

You can use a variety of tools to prepare your infusion, for example, a teacup with a lid, a teapot, a mason jar, etc. Just remember that your vessel must have a lid to keep the amount of volatile essential oils in the water from evaporating. Infusions can be both hot or cold, and they can be kept in the refrigerator for up to 24 hours.

How to Prepare a Hot Infusion

Pour 1.5 cups of hot water over 1 or 2 tablespoons of your tea blend. Then, allow it to steep by covering the vessel. It takes about 15 to 20 minutes for most herbal teas to steep. You can also choose to steep your tea for 5 to 10 minutes and then steep it again later. To avoid the bitter tannins in black or green tea blends, you should steep for only 5 minutes.

How to Prepare a Cold Infusion

In a closed container, combine 1 tablespoon tea with 1 cup cold water. After a few seconds of shaking, place the container in a cool area for at least 2 hours. Ingredients that work well in cold extractions include raspberry leaf, fruits, slippery elm, and marshmallow root.

Decoctions

A decoction is a procedure in which rough plant parts, including stems, bark, roots, and seeds, are put in a container with cold water, covered, and gradually heated to a boil. Plants must be started in cold water because tougher plant portions contain more albumin, a protein that must be slowly removed from cells as the water temperature rises.

How to Prepare a Decoction

In a covered saucepan, combine a tablespoon of ingredients per cup of cold water. If you have enough time, you can macerate the herbs in cool water for a few hours to soften up the dried plant material. Bring the herbs to a boil, then remove from heat. Allow 20 to 45 minutes for the herbs to cool and then strain.

How to Prepare Sun Tea

This is another great magical option. To make sun tea, fill a jar with cold water and herbs and spices. Then put the lid on and shake vigorously for a few seconds.

Place the jar on a sunny windowsill for a few hours, making sure the herbs are completely soaked. Sun teas are vibrant and energetic, perfectly complementing the wildness of fresh herbs and great for enhancing your magic.

How to Prepare Chai Tea

To prepare the base for your chai tea, combine 1 cup of chai spice concentrate and 1 cup milk (or water) in a covered pot.

Warm over medium heat only - be careful not to boil or it will scald the milk. Once the mixture is hot, remove from heat and add 1 teaspoon black tea leaves and 1 teaspoon honey. Steep for up to 6 minutes, then strain and serve.

Chai Concentrate Recipes

In the following pages you will find are a variety of recipes for different chai spice concentrates. However, remember that chai tea doesn't have to be something super elaborate or complicated. You can prepare it by simply including a bit of cardamom or cinnamon in your cup of black tea.

In general, for chai concentrate recipes, use the ingredients specified in each recipe and follow this brewing process:

> For every 1 cup of water, use 2 tablespoons of spice mix. In a covered pot, combine the spices and cool water. Bring to a low boil and cook for up to 40 minutes, occasionally stirring to prevent the water from boiling over. Keep the saucepan covered to prevent both water and essential oils from evaporating. Then, follow the instructions above to prepare your chai tea.

Finally, to make an iced chai, mix 1 cup chai strained concentrate and 1 cup milk (or water). Serve over ice.

How to Enhance the Energy of Fresh Herbs

Overall, most teas can be made using dried or fresh herbs. Actually, I like using both kinds of herbs, and I personally consider that magic and spells are effective both ways. However, if you choose to use fresh herbs (maybe you grow them in your own garden), you should consider how to get the strongest energy from your plants.

For example, the plant expends a lot of energy on leaf growth in the spring; therefore, making magic tea in the spring is most powerful when using the leaves rather than stems or roots, or any early, lone blossoms.

Flowers should be harvested when they are in bud or just before they reach their peak. Fruits are most beneficial when they are fully ripe, and seeds are best to gather when they are about to fall off the plant. Harvest roots in the fall or early spring following winter dormancy because that's when the plant's energy has withdrawn there.

Although this rule of thumb can truly help you boost your magic, consider that there are many exceptions. For example, in the case of many annual plants, you can harvest the entire plant at once.

Tips for Using Fresh Herbs

Hot Infusion with Fresh Herbs:

Dried herbs are frequently offered to you already sliced and sifted. When using fresh herbs, you should rip them lightly or finely chop them using a knife. If you want a strong tea, you'll need to completely fill your vessel with fresh herbs due to their high water content. Fil your cup, teapot or jar full to the brim with herbs, pour hot water on top, cover, and leave to steep until your tea is cool enough.

Cold Infusion with Fresh Herbs:

Fill your container with herbs and cold water, ensuring that the herbs are completely submerged. Then cover the vessel and shake it for a few seconds before placing it in a cool area. Allow to steep for many hours or even overnight.

Tea Witchcraft Recipes

Basic Instructions

Please keep in mind that all the measurements of the following recipes are approximate. To make any of the below recipes (or any recipe in general), use a single tablespoon of the dry mix inside a tea ball or cheesecloth filter to produce a standard cup of tea (approximately 250 milliliters or 8 ounces). In general, all liquid measures should be added according to taste. Unless otherwise indicated, allow between 5 and 15 minutes for the magical infusion to steep or longer if you desire a stronger flavor.

Many of the recipes in this book are written in "parts" so that you can change and adapt them depending on your specific requirements. (Some others are not because they were transmitted to me this way, and I have chosen to respect the magical proportions they were created with. However, you can, of course, decide to change those quantities to scale your recipe up or down.) If a recipe indicates "parts" as the unit of measurement, you will just have to select how much tea you want to prepare before you begin.

Let's say that you want to make 2 pounds (32 ounces) of a magic tea mixture and the recipe calls for:

- 1.5 parts black tea
- 1 part rose petals
- 1 part raspberry leaf
- 0.5 part fennel

First, you need to calculate how many ounces there are in a single part. You can do that by summing up the total parts in the recipe. In this case, 1.5 + 1 + 1 + 0.5 = 4 parts. And because you want to prepare 32 ounces of magic tea, you will have to divide 32 by 4. So, each part is 8 ounces, which means you will have to multiply each part of your recipe by this number to determine how much of each by weight. Easy, isn't it?

You can also simply choose some measuring device to be your "part" and use that according to the recipe. So if you use a coffee mug as your measuring device, you would put 1 full mug and another half of a mug of black tea into your mix, 1 full mug of rose petals, 1 full mug of raspberry leaf, and half a mug of fennel.

Think of "part" as a replacement for "cup", but you aren't limited to the specific size of standard measuring cup. You can use a soup pot as your "part" if you really want (and have a lot of tea and herbs!).

Last but not least, besides always testing for possible allergic reactions, remember to consult a physician, specialist pharmacist, or botanist before taking herbal remedies for an extended period. And NEVER consume any herb without consulting your doctor first in case of being pregnant, breastfeeding, or taking other medications or supplements.

Magical Recipes for...

Spiritual and Physical Health

1. Deep Wellness

Ingredients:

- 1 part elderberry
- 1 part echinacea
- 1 part elecampane root
- 1 part spearmint
- 1 part eucalyptus
- 1 part lemon balm
- 0.5 part yerba santa
- 0.5 part licorice root

Pour 1.5 cups of hot water on 1 tablespoon of tea mixture.
Steep for up to 10 minutes.

2. Uplift your Spirit

Ingredients:

- 4 parts honeybush
- 3 parts cinnamon
- 1.5 parts cardamom
- 1.5 parts ginger
- 1 part orange zest
- 1 part clove
- 0.35 part licorice root

Pour 1.5 cups of hot water on 1 tablespoon of tea mixture.
Steep for up to 10 minutes.

3. Overcome Gray Days

Ingredients:

- 1 part Earl Grey tea
- 0.5 part lemongrass
- 0.25 part rose petals
- 1 dried and chopped vanilla bean per pound (16 ounces) of tea mixture

Pour 1.5 cups of hot water on 1 tablespoon of tea mixture.
Steep for up to 10 minutes.

4. Reconnect with Your own Breath

Ingredients:

- 1 part yerba maté
- 0.5 part elderberry
- 0.5 part peppermint
- 0.5 part lemongrass
- 0.25 part yerba santa
- 0.25 part linden

Pour 1.5 cups of hot water on 1 tablespoon of tea mixture.
Steep for up to 10 minutes.

5. Mental Clarity

Ingredients:

- 2 parts white tea
- 1 part rose hips
- 0.5 part cinnamon
- 0.5 part ginger
- 0.5 part lemongrass
- 0.25 part orange zest
- 0.25 part lemon balm

Pour 1.5 cups of hot water on 1 tablespoon of tea mixture.
Steep for up to 10 minutes.

6. Open Your Eyes

Ingredients:

- 2 parts keemun tea
- 2 parts orange zest
- 1.5 parts rose hips
- 1.5 parts hawthorn leaf and flower
- 1 part lemongrass
- 1 part hawthorn berries
- 1 part anise seeds
- 1 part cinnamon
- 1 part nettle leaf

Pour 1.5 cups of hot water on 1 tablespoon of tea mixture. Steep for up to 10 minutes.

7. Awaken your Mind

Ingredients:

- 2 parts gotu kola
- 1.5 parts tulsi
- 1 part licorice root
- 1 part peppermint
- 1 part green rooibos
- 1 part sage

Pour 1.5 cups of hot water on 1 tablespoon of tea mixture. Steep for up to 10 minutes.

8. Rebuild the Emotional Heart

Ingredients:

- 1 part linden
- 1 part mint
- 1 part hawthorn leaf
- 1 part hawthorn berry
- 1 part red sage root

- 1 part nettle leaf
- 0.5 part osmanthus flowers

Pour 1.5 cups of hot water on 1 tablespoon of tea mixture. Steep for up to 10 minutes.

9. Stronger Self

Ingredients:

- 1 part linden
- 1 part fennel
- 1 part lemon balm
- 1 part goji berries
- 0.5 part chamomile
- 0.25 part licorice root

Pour 1.5 cups of hot water on 1 tablespoon of tea mixture. Steep for up to 10 minutes.

10. Feel Calm and Secure

Ingredients:

- 1 part chamomile
- 1 part passionflower
- 1 part mint
- 1 part fennel
- 0.5 part lemon balm
- 0.5 part rose hips
- 0.25 part marshmallow leaves

Pour 1.5 cups of hot water on 1 tablespoon of tea mixture. Steep for up to 10 minutes.

11. Breathe Again

Ingredients:

- 3 parts fennel seeds

- 3 parts ginger
- 3 parts peppermint
- 3 parts eucalyptus
- 2 parts hyssop
- 1 part clove
- 1 part elecampane root

Pour 1.5 cups of hot water on 1 tablespoon of tea mixture. Steep for up to 10 minutes.

12. Feel Your Inner Power

Ingredients:

- 4 parts rose hips
- 3 parts cinnamon
- 2 parts wild cherry bark
- 2 parts licorice root
- 2 parts fennel
- 2 parts marshmallow root

Pour 1.5 cups of hot water on 1 tablespoon of tea mixture. Steep for up to 10 minutes.

13. Rouse the Senses

Ingredients:

- 3 parts mint
- 2 parts damiana
- 2 parts cacao nibs
- 1.5 parts rosehips
- 1.5 parts cinnamon
- 1 part passionflower
- 0.25 part licorice root

Pour 1.5 cups of hot water on 1 tablespoon of tea mixture. Steep for up to 10 minutes.

14. Good Health

Ingredients:

- 1 tablespoon black tea
- 2 tablespoons hops
- 2 tablespoons fennel
- 1 tablespoon elderberry
- 1 tablespoon mint

Pour 1.5 cups of hot water on 1 tablespoon of tea mixture.
Steep for up to 10 minutes.

15. Happiness

Ingredients:

- 1 tablespoon lavender
- 1 tablespoon red clover
- 1/4 teaspoon marjoram
- 1 teaspooon honey
- A few lemon slices to serve

Mix the first three ingredients.
Pour 1.5 cups of hot water on 1 tablespoon of tea mixture.
Steep for up to 10 minutes.
Serve with honey and a slice of lemon in each cup.

16. Wisdom

Ingredients:

- 1 teaspoon black tea
- 2 tablespoons dried peach pieces
- 1 teaspoon dried sage
- 2 teaspoons honey
- 1 slice of lemon

Mix the first three ingredients.
Pour 1.5 cups of hot water on 1 tablespoon of tea mixture.
Steep for up to 10 minutes.

Serve with honey and a slice of lemon in each cup.

17. Cleanse your Aura

Ingredients:

- 1/4 teaspoon thyme
- 1/4 teaspoon lemon balm
- 1/4 teaspoon dandelion

Pour 1.5 cups of hot water on 1 tablespoon of tea mixture.
Steep for up to 10 minutes.

18. Instill Peace throughout your Being

Ingredients:

- 1 teaspoon violet blossoms
- 1 teaspoon passionflower
- 3 sprigs of fresh thyme
- 1 teaspoon honey

Mix the first three ingredients.
Pour 1.5 cups of hot water on 1 tablespoon of tea mixture.
Steep for up to 10 minutes.
Serve with honey to taste.

19. Cleanse the Energies

Ingredients:

- 1 tablespoon dried lemon peel
- 1 teaspoon lemon verbena
- 1 teaspoon vervain
- 1 teaspoon coconut sugar
- 1 sprig fresh rosemary
- A few drops of coconut milk

Mix the first three ingredients.
Pour 1.5 cups of hot water on 1 tablespoon of tea mixture.

Steep for up to 10 minutes.
Serve with coconut sugar and coconut milk to taste, and rosemary as a garnish.

20. Keep Anxiety Away

Ingredients:

- 1 teaspoon mint
- 1 teaspoon geranium leaves and flowers
- 1 sprig thyme
- 1 sprig marjoram
- A few drops of lemon juice

Mix the first two ingredients.
Pour 1.5 cups of hot water on 1 tablespoon of tea mixture.
Steep for up to 10 minutes.
Serve with lemon juice to taste, and thyme and marjoram as a garnish.

21. Longevity and Wisdom

Ingredients:

- 1 tablespoon dried lemon peel
- 1 tablespoon dried apple slices
- 1 teaspoon lavender
- 1 teaspoon sage
- 1 teaspoon rose hips

Pour 1.5 cups of hot water on 1 tablespoon of tea mixture.
Steep for up to 10 minutes.

22. Cleanse the Chakras

Ingredients:

- 1 teaspoon peppermint
- 1 teaspoon hibiscus
- ¼ tsp lemongrass

- 1/8 teaspoon mugwort
- 1 teaspoon coconut sugar
- 1 sprig of fresh rosemary

Mix the first four ingredients.
Pour 1.5 cups of hot water on 1 tablespoon of tea mixture.
Steep for up to 10 minutes.
Serve with coconut sugar to taste, and rosemary as a garnish.

23. Stay Focused

Ingredients:

- 1 teaspoon mint
- 1 teaspoon lemon verbena
- 1 dash yellow mustard seed
- 1 teaspoon honey
- 1 sprig of fresh rosemary
- 1 slice of fresh lemon

Mix the first three ingredients.
Pour 1.5 cups of hot water on 1 tablespoon of tea mixture.
Steep for up to 10 minutes.
Serve with honey and lemon slices to taste, and rosemary as a garnish.

24. Quick Cleansing

Ingredients:

- 1 part black tea
- 1 part bergamot
- A squeeze of fresh lemon

Mix first two ingredients.
Pour 1.5 cups of hot water on 1 tablespoon of tea mixture.
Steep for up to 10 minutes.
Serve with a squeeze of fresh lemon juice.

25. Boost Your Immunity

Ingredients:

- ½ teaspoon ground turmeric
- ½ teaspoon ground ginger
- 1 lemon wedge
- 1 tablespoon maple syrup

Mix first two ingredients.
Pour 1.5 cups of hot water on 1 tablespoon of tea mixture.
Steep for up to 10 minutes.
Serve with maple syrup to taste and garnish with lemon wedge.

26. Say Goodbye to Bad Thoughts

Ingredients:

- ½ cup of fresh mint leaves
- 1 tablespoon lavender petals
- 1 teaspoon honey

Mix first two ingredients.
Pour 1.5 cups of hot water on 1 tablespoon of tea mixture.
Steep for up to 10 minutes.
Serve with honey to taste.

27. Cure your Soul

Ingredients:

- 1 teaspoon black tea
- 1 teaspoon nettle
- 1 teaspoon elderberry
- 1 teaspoon rosehips
- 1 teaspoon burdock

Pour 1.5 cups of hot water on 1 tablespoon of tea mixture.
Steep for up to 10 minutes.

28. Meditation

Ingredients:

- 1 teaspoon black tea
- 1 teaspoon chamomile
- 1 teaspoon elderberry
- 1 teaspoon rose hips

Pour 1.5 cups of hot water on 1 tablespoon of tea mixture.
Steep for up to 10 minutes.

29. Improve Your Health

Ingredients:

- 1 tablespoon black tea
- 1 tablespoon dried mint
- 1 tablespoon elderberry
- 2 tablespoons rose hips
- 2 tablespoons hops
- 2 tablespoons fennel
- A bit of cinnamon

Pour 1.5 cups of hot water on 1 tablespoon of tea.
Steep for up to 10 minutes.

30. Leave Sadness Behind

Ingredients:

- 3 cloves
- 10 grams raisins
- A slice of apple
- A slice of fresh lemon
- A slice of orange
- A slice of ginger
- Half cinnamon stick

Mix all items in a small teapot or large cup – this only makes one cup of tea.

Pour 1.5 cups of hot water on entire tea mixture.
Steep for up to 10 minutes.

31. Boost the Body and Spirit

Ingredients:

- 3 parts fenugreek seeds
- 2 parts mint
- 2 parts oat straw
- 2 parts goji berries
- 2 parts milky oat tops
- 1 part anise seeds
- 1 part alfalfa
- 1 part nettle leaf

Pour 1.5 cups of hot water on 2 tablespoons of tea mixture.
Steep for up to 15 minutes.

32. Boost your Inner Strenght

Ingredients:

- 1 part nettle leaf
- 1 part raspberry leaf
- 1.5 parts peppermint
- 0.5 part rose petals
- 0.5 part fennel

Pour 1.5 cups of hot water on 2 tablespoons of tea mixture.
Steep for up to 15 minutes.

33. Make the Pain Go Away

Ingredients:

- 1 part skullcap
- 1 part fennel
- 1 part corydalis
- 0.5 part wild yam

- 0.5 part mint
- 0.25 part licorice root

Pour 1.5 cups of hot water on 2 tablespoons of tea mixture.
Steep for up to 15 minutes.

34. Great Energy

Ingredients:

- 1 part lemon leaves
- 1 part chamomile flowers
- 1 part St. John's wort leaves
- 1 part hawthorn leaves, berries, and blossoms
- 1/8 part lavender flower
- 2 drops of ginseng tincture

Mix the first five ingredients.
Pour 1.5 cups of hot water on 2 tablespoons of tea mixture.
Steep for up to 15 minutes.
Add the ginseng tincture to the last few sips of infusion.

35. Healing

Ingredients:

- 2 parts angelica
- 1/2 part black cohosh
- 1/2 part sage
- A pinch of rosemary

Pour 1.5 cups of hot water on 2 tablespoons of tea mixture.
Steep for up to 15 minutes.

36. Spirituality

Ingredients:

- 1 part hibiscus
- 1 part linden

- 2 tablespoons milk
- A few drops of cranberry juice

Mix first two ingredients.
Pour 1.5 cups of hot water on 2 tablespoons of tea mixture.
Steep for up to 15 minutes.
Add milk and cranberry juice just before serving.

37. Joyful Spirit:

Ingredients:

- 2 parts verbena
- 1 part dried orange peel
- 2 lemon leaves
- ¼ slice of orange
- A few flakes of cinnamon stick

Pour 1.5 cups of hot water on 2 tablespoons of tea mixture.
Steep for up to 15 minutes.

38. Female Health

Ingredients:

- 5 parts pau d'arco
- 2 parts milky oat tops
- 1 part mint
- 1 part thyme
- 1 part calendula
- 0.5 part clove
- 0.5 part oregano

Pour 1.5 cups of hot water on 2 tablespoons of tea mixture.
Steep for up to 15 minutes.

39. When Trying to Conceive

Ingredients:

- 2 parts raspberry leaf
- 2 parts nettle leaf
- 2 parts rose petals
- 2 parts peppermint
- 1 part chamomile
- 1 part oat straw
- 1 part dandelion leaf
- 1 part alfalfa

Pour 1.5 cups of hot water on 2 tablespoons of tea mixture.
Steep for up to 15 minutes.

40. Fertility

Ingredients:

- 2 parts ginseng
- 1/2 part of mugwort
- A pinch of savory
- A little bit of a non-citrus juice

Mix the first three ingredients.
Pour 1.5 cups of hot water on 2 tablespoons of tea mixture.
Steep for up to 15 minutes.
Add juice before serving.

41. Youthful Appearance

Ingredients:

- 3 parts milky oat tops
- 2 parts elderberry
- 2 parts rose hips
- 1 part orange peel
- 1 part goji berry
- 1 part lemongrass
- 0.5 part hibiscus

- 0.25 part licorice

Pour 1.5 cups of hot water on 2 tablespoons of tea mixture. Steep for up to 15 minutes.

42. Mental Clarity and Balance

Ingredients:

- 3 parts tulsi
- 1 part cardamom
- 1 part peppermint
- 1 part cinnamon
- 0.5 part gotu kola
- 0.5 part rose petals

Pour 1.5 cups of hot water on 2 tablespoons of tea mixture. Steep for up to 15 minutes.

43. Awaken your Senses

Ingredients:

- 1.25 parts green tea
- 1 part lemongrass
- 0.75 part tulsi
- 0.5 part chamomile
- 0.5 part gotu kola

Pour 1.5 cups of hot water on 2 tablespoons of tea mixture. Steep for up to 15 minutes.

44. Overcome a Stressful Experience

Ingredients:

- 1.5 parts mint
- 1.5 parts fennel
- 1 part rose petals
- 1 part chamomile

- 1 part nettle leaf
- 1 part skullcap
- 0.5 part catnip
- 0.5 part raspberry leaf
- A touch of honey

Mix first eight ingredients.
Pour 1.5 cups of hot water on 2 tablespoons of tea mixture.
Steep for up to 15 minutes.
Add honey to taste.

45. Body and Soul Wellness

Ingredients:

- 1 part rose hips
- 1 part nettle leaf
- 1 part ginger
- 1 part milky oat tops
- 1 part oat straw
- 0.5 part lemongrass
- 0.5 part chamomile
- 0.25 part rosemary

Pour 1.5 cups of hot water on 2 tablespoons of tea mixture.
Steep for up to 15 minutes.

46. Calm your Soul

Ingredients:

- 1.25 parts chamomile
- 1 part mint
- 1 part catnip
- 1 part skullcap
- 0.3 part licorice root
- 0.25 part hops

Pour 1.5 cups of hot water on 2 tablespoons of tea mixture.
Steep for up to 15 minutes.

47. Rejuvenate your Soul

Ingredients:

- 5 parts burdock root
- 3 parts fenugreek seeds
- 3 parts dandelion root
- 2.5 parts codonopsis
- 2 parts rhodiola
- 2 parts chaga mushrooms
- 2 parts astragalus
- 1 part reishi mushrooms

In a lidded saucepan, mix 3 tablespoons tea mixture and 4 cups water.

Slowly bring to a simmer and continue for up to 60 minutes.

48. Overcome Sluggish Days

Ingredients:

- 1 part black tea
- 1 part nettle leaf
- 1 part fennel
- 0.5 part rose petals
- 0.5 part mint

Pour 1.5 cups of hot water on 1 tablespoon of tea mixture.
Steep for about 3 minutes and strain.
Then steep again for 3 more minutes.

49. Restore the Nursing Mother

Ingredients:

- 10 parts fenugreek seeds
- 5 parts fennel
- 5 parts mint
- 4 parts nettle leaf
- 2 parts lemon balm
- 2 parts chamomile

- 2 parts alfalfa

Pour 1 cup of hot water on 1 tablespoon of tea mixture.
Steep for up to 15 minutes.

50. New Mothers' Care

Ingredients:

- 2 parts lemon balm
- 2 parts gotu kola
- 1 part milky oat tops
- 1 part nettle leaf
- 1 part chamomile

Pour 1 cup of hot water on 1 tablespoon of tea mixture.
Steep for up to 15 minutes.

51. Fight Anxiety

Ingredients:

- 2 parts mint
- 2 parts senna
- 1 part fennel
- 0.5 part ground cinnamon
- 1 dried prune per cup
- 0.5 tablespoon grated fresh ginger per cup

Mix first 4 ingredients.
Pour 1 cup hot water over 1 tablespoon herb mix, prune, and ginger.
Steep for 15 minutes.

52. Overcome a Bad Experience of Any Kind

Ingredients:

- 1 part kukicha twig tea
- 1 part rosehips

- 1 part fennel
- 1 part codonopsis
- 1 part chaga mushrooms
- 1 part astragalus

In a covered pot, combine 1 teaspoons of tea mixture and 1 cups of cold water.

Bring the water to a gentle simmer without allowing it to boil over.

Allow to simmer for at least 20 minutes over low heat. Strain and consume.

53. Finally Heal

Ingredients:

- 1 teaspoon saffron
- ½ cup apple cider
- 1 stick of cinnamon
- 1 teaspoon honey

In a half cup of hot water, steep the saffron and cinnamon stick.

Honey can be added to taste.

When the tea has slightly cooled, stir in the apple cider.

54. Feel Active and Strong

Ingredients:

- 2 parts cinnamon
- 2 parts chaga mushrooms
- 1 part Asian ginseng
- 1 part reishi mushrooms
- 1 part astragalus
- 1 part fresh ginger
- 1 part fennel

In a covered pot, combine 1 teaspoon of tea mixture and 1 cup of cold water.

Bring the water to a gentle simmer without allowing it to boil over.

Allow to simmer for about 20 minutes over low heat.

55. Women's Strength

Ingredients:

- 1.5 parts rose hips
- 1 part cinnamon
- 1 part burdock root
- 1 part dandelion root
- 1 part astragalus
- 1 part ginger
- 0.5 part orange peel
- 0.25 part clove

In a covered pot, combine 1 teaspoon of tea mixture and 1 cup of cold water.

Bring the water to a gentle simmer without allowing it to boil over.

Allow to simmer for about 20 minutes over low heat.

56. Glow

Ingredients:

- 1 part burdock root
- 1 part dandelion root
- 0.5 part nettle leaf
- 0.25 part licorice root
- 0.15 part calendula flowers

In a covered pot, combine 1 teaspoon of tea mixture and 1 cup of cold water.

Bring the water to a gentle simmer without allowing it to boil over.

Allow to simmer for about 20 minutes over low heat.

57. Energize your Spirit

Ingredients:

- 1 teaspoon raspberries
- 1 teaspoon mint
- 1 teaspoon echinacea
- 1 teaspoon lemon balm

- 1 teaspoon rose hips
- 1 teaspoon thyme

If using fresh raspberries, mix all other ingredients together.

Pour 1.5 cups of hot water on 1 tablespoon of tea mixture. Add fresh raspberries to steeping tea if mixture does not include dried raspberries.

Steep for up to 10 minutes.

Sleep and Dreams

58. Restful Sleep

Ingredients:

- 1 teaspoon valerian root
- 1 teaspoon thyme
- 1 teaspoon elderberries
- 1 teaspoon passionflower

Pour 1.5 cups of hot water on 1 tablespoon of tea mixture.
Steep for up to 10 minutes.

59. Sleep like the Gods

Ingredients:

- 2 parts valerian
- 1 part mint
- 1 part linden
- 1 part passionflower
- 0.25 part nutmeg
- 0.25 part hops

Pour 1.5 cups of hot water on 1 tablespoon of tea mixture.
Steep for up to 10 minutes.

60. Prophetic Dreams

Ingredients:

- 1 teaspoon blue mallow
- 1 teaspoon mullein
- ¼ teaspoon mugwort
- ¼ teaspoon goldenrod
- 2 teaspoons honey

Mix first four ingredients.
Pour 1.5 cups of hot water on 1 tablespoon of tea mixture.
Steep for up to 10 minutes.
Add honey to taste.

61. Sweet Dreams:

Ingredients:

- 1 tablespoon of peppermint
- 1 tablespoon of mugwort
- ½ part ground cinnamon
- 2 leaves of jasmine flowers
- 2 rose petals

Pour 1.5 cups of hot water on 1 tablespoon of tea mixture.
Steep for up to 10 minutes.

62. Astral Dreams

Ingredients:

- 1 part of valerian
- 1 part spearmint
- 1 part of ginko
- 1 part of mugwort
- A bit of allspice
- A few drops of extract of aniseed

Mix the first five ingredients.
Pour 1.5 cups of hot water on 2 tablespoons of tea mixture.
Steep for up to 15 minutes.
Add aniseed extract right before serving.

63. Magical Dreams

Ingredients:

- 1 part valerian root
- 3 parts peppermint
- A pinch of euphrasia
- A pinch of ground ginger

Mix first three ingredients.
Pour 1.5 cups of hot water on 2 tablespoons of tea mixture.
Add ginger and steep for up to 15 minutes.

Divination and Magic

64. Novice Witch

Ingredients:

- 1 part green tea
- 0.5 part toasted coconut

Pour 1.5 cups of hot water on 1 tablespoon of tea mixture.
Steep for about 2 minutes and then strain.
Steep three more times again for 2 more minutes each.

65. Divination:

Ingredients:

- 1 tablespoon black tea
- 1 tablespoon mugwort
- 1 tablespoon Euphrasia
- 2 tablespoons lemon juice

Mix first three ingredients.
Pour 1.5 cups of hot water on 1 tablespoon of tea mixture.
Steep for up to 10 minutes.
Add lemon juice before serving.

66. New Moon

Ingredients:

- 2 teaspoons lavender
- 1 teaspoon milk thistle
- 1 teaspoon dried elderberries
- 1 teaspoon vetiver

Pour 1.5 cups of hot water on 2 tablespoons of tea mixture.
Steep for up to 15 minutes.

67. Wise Witch of the Woods

Ingredients:

- 1 part kukicha twig tea
- 1 part nettle leaf
- 1 part lapsang souchong
- 1 part cedar tips
- 0.5 part jasmine flowers

Pour 1.5 cups of hot water on 1 tablespoon of tea mixture.
Steep for up to 10 minutes.

68. Honor a Long-Gone Witch

Ingredients:

- 2 parts green tea
- 2 parts roasted almonds
- 1 part cardamom
- 1 part rose petals
- 0.5 part ground cinnamon

Pour 1.5 cups of hot water on 1 tablespoon of tea mixture.
Steep for up to 10 minutes.

69. Spicy Witches

Ingredients:

- 1 part ginger
- 1 part tulsi
- 1 part mint
- 0.5 part echinacea
- 0.5 part lemongrass
- 0.1 part cayenne

Pour 1.5 cups of hot water on 1 tablespoon of tea mixture.
Steep for up to 10 minutes.

70. Allow your Mind to Travel to the Past

Ingredients:

- 2 parts rose hips
- 2 parts elderberry
- 2 parts honeybush
- 1.5 parts rose petals
- 1 part lemongrass
- 1 part lavender blossoms

Pour 1.5 cups of hot water on 1 tablespoon of tea mixture.
Steep for up to 10 minutes.

71. Revive a Lost Memory

Ingredients:

- 2 parts honeybush
- 1 part peppermint
- 1 part spearmint
- 1 dried and chopped vanilla bean per pound of blended tea
- Fresh lemon zest

Mix first four ingredients.
Pour 1.5 cups of hot water on 1 tablespoon of tea mixture.
Steep for up to 10 minutes.
Add lemon zest to each cup before serving.

72. Dark Desire

Ingredients:

- 1 part black tea
- 1 part fresh mint
- 0.5 part rose petals

Pour 1.5 cups of hot water on 1 tablespoon of tea mixture.
Steep for up to 10 minutes.

73. Powerful Rituals

Ingredients:

- 1 part nettle leaf
- 1 part mint
- 1 part fennel
- 1 part raspberry leaf
- 0.5 part rose petals
- 0.5 part ginger

Pour 1.5 cups of hot water on 1 tablespoon of tea mixture.
Steep for up to 10 minutes.

74. Awaken your Psychic Abilities

Ingredients:

- 1 teaspoon peppermint
- 1 teaspoon lemon balm
- 1 teaspoon yarrow
- 1 stick of cinnamon
- ½ teaspoon mugwort

- ¼ teaspoon whole cloves

Pour 1.5 cups of hot water on 1 tablespoon of tea mixture.
Place cinnamon stick in each cup.
Steep for up to 10 minutes.

75. Clairvoyance Rituals

Ingredients:

- 1 tablespoon dried orange peel
- 1 tablespoon dried fig
- 1 teaspoon hibiscus
- 1 teaspoon dandelion root
- A pinch of mugwort
- 1 teaspoon honey

Mix first five ingredients.
Pour 1.5 cups of hot water on 1 tablespoon of tea mixture.
Steep for up to 10 minutes.
Add honey before serving.

76. Sharpen Your Magical Senses

Ingredients:

- 1 teaspoon black tea
- 1 tablespoon dried cherries
- 1 teaspoon peppermint

Pour 1.5 cups of hot water on 1 tablespoon of tea mixture.
Steep for up to 10 minutes.

77. Break a Spell

Ingredients:

- 1 teaspoon blue vervain
- 1 teaspoon hawthorn berries
- 1 teaspoon rose hips

- 1 teaspoon almond milk

Mix first three ingredients.
Pour 1.5 cups of hot water on 1 tablespoon of tea mixture.
Steep for up to 10 minutes.
Add almond milk before serving.

78. See the Truth

Ingredients:
- 1 teaspoon dandelion root
- 1 teaspoon dandelion leaf
- 2 teaspoons borage flowers
- 2 teaspoons red clover
- 1 teaspoon almond milk

Mix first four ingredients.
Pour 1.5 cups of hot water on 1 tablespoon of tea mixture.
Steep for up to 10 minutes.
Add almond milk before serving.

79. Divination Spells

Ingredients:
- 1 teaspoon oolong tea
- 1 teaspoon marshmallow root
- 1 teaspoon willow bark
- 1 teaspoon coconut sugar
- 1 teaspoon coconut milk

Mix first three ingredients.
Pour 1.5 cups hot water on 1 tablespoon of tea mixture.
Steep for up to 10 minutes.
Add coconut sugar and coconut milk before serving.

80. For a Special Spell

Ingredients:

- 1 teaspoon black tea
- 1 teaspoon dandelion root
- 1 star anise
- 1 stick cinnamon
- 2 teaspoons date sugar
- 1 teaspoon hazelnut milk

Mix first two ingredients.
Pour 1.5 cups of hot water on 1 tablespoon of tea mixture.
Place star anise and cinnamon stick in each cup.
Steep for up to 10 minutes.
Add hazelnut milk before serving.

81. New Beginnings

Ingredients:

- 3 pieces of dried ginger
- 1 part lemongrass
- A smidgeon of dill
- A squeeze of lemon

Mix first three ingredients.
Pour 1.5 cups of hot water on 2 tablespoons of tea mixture.
Steep for up to 15 minutes.
Add lemon juice before serving.

82. Feminine Mysteries

Ingredients:

- 2 parts willow bark
- A pinch of rosemary
- A few drops of apple juice
- 1 tablespoon vanilla extract

Mix the first two ingredients.

Pour 1.5 cups of hot water on 2 tablespoons of tea mixture.
Steep for up to 15 minutes.
Add apple juice and vanilla extract before serving.

83. Connect with the Deities

Ingredients:

- 2 tablespoons black tea
- ½ tablespoon elderberry
- ½ teaspoon chamomile

Pour 1.5 cups of hot water on 2 tablespoons of tea mixture.
Steep for up to 15 minutes.

84. Prophecies

Ingredients:

- 1 part kelp (seaweed)
- 1/2 part raspberry
- 1/2 part rose petals
- A pinch of yarrow

Pour 1.5 cups of hot water on 2 tablespoons of tea mixture.
Steep for up to 15 minutes.

85. Start a New Magic Practice

Ingredients:

- 2 parts kukicha twig tea
- 1.5 parts ginger
- 1 part mint
- 1 part ground cinnamon
- 0.75 part cardamom
- 0.75 part chaga mushrooms
- 0.75 part fennel
- 0.5 part codonopsis
- 0.25 part ground clove

Pour 1.5 cups of hot water on 2 tablespoons of tea mixture.
Steep for up to 15 minutes.

86. Honor Someone's Magic

Ingredients:

- 3 parts cacao skins
- 3 parts honeybush
- 1 part peppermint
- 1 part nettle leaf
- 1 dried and chopped vanilla bean per pound of tea
- 1 drop jasmine essential oil

Mix first five ingredients.
Pour 1.5 cups of hot water on 1 tablespoon of tea mixture.
Steep for up to 10 minutes.
Add jasmine oil to each cup before serving.

Work, Abundance, and Success

87. Relieve Work Frustration

Ingredients:

- 1 part raspberry leaf
- 1 part nettle leaf
- 1 part skullcap
- 1 part catnip
- 1 part rose petals
- 0.5 part rosehips
- 0.5 part chamomile
- 0.5 part hibiscus
- 1 dried and chopped vanilla bean per pound of tea

Pour 1.5 cups of hot water on 1 tablespoon of tea mixture.
Steep for up to 10 minutes.

88. Success at Work

Ingredients:

- 4 parts black tea
- 1 part lavender blossoms
- 1 part cardamom
- 1 dried and chopped vanilla bean per pound of tea

Pour 1.5 cups of hot water on 1 tablespoon of tea mixture. Steep for up to 10 minutes.

89. Abundance for the Whole Family

Ingredients:

- 3 parts hibiscus
- 2 parts dried berries
- 2 parts lemongrass
- 1 part linden

Pour 1.5 cups of hot water on 1 tablespoon of tea mixture. Steep for up to 10 minutes.

90. Express All your Potential

Ingredients:

- 4 parts rose hips
- 3 parts lemongrass
- 3 parts lemon balm
- 3 parts orange zest
- 3 parts ginger
- 2 parts cinnamon

Pour 1.5 cups of hot water on 1 tablespoon of tea mixture. Steep for up to 10 minutes.

91. Overcome Any Difficulty

Ingredients:

- 1 part ginger
- 1 part mint
- 1 part elderflower
- 0.5 part cinnamon
- 0.5 part cardamom
- 0.5 part yarrow

Pour 1.5 cups of hot water on 1 tablespoon of tea mixture.
Steep for up to 10 minutes.

92. Business Luck

Ingredients:

- 1 teaspoon black tea
- 1 tablespoon dried orange peel
- 1 teaspoon linden flowers
- 1 dash ground cinnamon
- 1 dash ground allspice
- 1 dash ground nutmeg
- 1 star anise
- 1teaspoon honey
- 2 teaspoons almond milk

Mix the first six ingredients.
Pour 1.5 cups of hot water on 1 tablespoon of tea mixture.
Place star anise in each cup.
Steep for up to 10 minutes.
Add honey and almond milk before serving.

93. Triumph

Ingredients:

- 1 teaspoon mullein
- 1 teaspoon vetiver
- 1 teaspoon lemon balm

- 1 teaspoon mint
- 1 teaspoon honey

Mix first four ingredients.
Pour 1.5 cups of hot water on 1 tablespoon of tea mixture.
Steep for up to 10 minutes.
Add honey before serving.

94. Face Challenges with Success

Ingredients:

- 1 teaspoon black tea
- 1 teaspoon chamomile
- 1 teaspoon yarrow
- 1 sprig of thyme
- 1 teaspoon of walnut milk

Mix first 3 ingredients.
Pour 1.5 cups of hot water on 1 tablespoon of tea mixture.
Steep for up to 10 minutes.
Add walnut milk and garnish with thyme before serving.

95. Abundance

Ingredients:

- 1 teaspoon green tea
- 1 teaspoon chickweed
- 1 teaspoon jasmine
- 1 tsp coconut milk

Mix first three ingredients.
Pour 1.5 cups of hot water on 1 tablespoon of tea mixture.
Steep for up to 10 minutes.
Add coconut milk before serving.

96. Everyday Luck

Ingredients:

- 1 part chamomile
- 1 part rose hips
- 1 part dried orange peel

Pour 1.5 cups of hot water on 1 tablespoon of tea mixture. Steep for up to 10 minutes.

97. Attract Wealth

Ingredients:

- 1 teaspoon chamomile
- 1 teaspoon goldenrod
- 1 teaspoon basil

Pour 1.5 cups of hot water on 1 tablespoon of tea mixture. Steep for up to 10 minutes.

98. Prosperity

Ingredients:

- 1 part catnip
- 1 part hawthorn
- 0.5 part chamomile
- 0.5 part rue

Pour 1.5 cups of hot water on 2 tablespoons of tea mixture. Steep for up to 15 minutes.

99. Strength and Endurance

Ingredients:

- 1.5 parts white oak bark
- 0.5 part orange peel
- 0.5 part mint

- A pinch of nutmeg

Pour 1.5 cups of hot water on 2 tablespoons of tea mixture.
Steep for up to 15 minutes.

100. Overcoming Difficulties

Ingredients:

- 1 part dandelion
- 1 part blackberry
- A pinch of hibiscus
- A few drops of red wine

Mix first three ingredients.
Pour 1.5 cups of hot water on 2 tablespoons of tea mixture.
Steep for up to 15 minutes.
Add red wine to each cup before serving.

101. Success in Cooperation

Ingredients:

- 1 part mullein
- 0.5 part barberry
- 0.25 part eucalyptus

Pour 1.5 cups of hot water on 2 tablespoons of tea mixture.
Steep for up to 15 minutes.

102. Stay Strong No Matter What

Ingredients:

- 1 part dandelion root
- 1 part burdock root
- 0.5 part ground cinnamon
- 0.5 part ground ginger
- 0.25 part reishi mushrooms
- 0.25 part licorice root

In a lidded saucepan, combine 2 tablespoons tea mixture and 4 cups water at room temperature.

Simmer over low heat for up to 60 minutes and strain.

103. Achieve your Wildest Dream

Ingredients:

- 2.5 parts black tea
- 1 part dried shiso
- 0.75 part mint
- 0.25 part licorice root
- A pinch of fresh lemon zest

Pour 1.5 cups of hot water on 1 tablespoon of tea mixture.
Steep for up to 10 minutes.

104. Safe and Succesful Travels

Ingredients:

- 10 parts black tea
- 3 parts cinnamon
- 2 parts rosemary
- 2 parts sage
- 2 parts winter savory
- 2 parts thyme

Pour 1.5 cups of hot water on 1 tablespoon of tea mixture.
Steep for up to 10 minutes.

Protection

105. Protect Your Home

Ingredients:

- 10 parts kukicha twig tea
- 5 parts cinnamon
- 3 parts codonopsis

- 3 parts orange peel
- 3 parts cardamom
- 2 parts clove
- 1 part licorice root

Pour 1.5 cups of hot water on 1 tablespoon of tea mixture. Steep for up to 10 minutes.

106. Protect your Loved Ones

Ingredients:

- 1 teaspoon blackberry leaf
- 1teaspoon pine needles
- 1 teaspoon dried elderberries

Pour 1.5 cups of hot water on 1 tablespoon of tea mixture. Steep for up to 10 minutes.

107. Protection from an Enemy

Ingredients:

- 6 parts ginger
- 6 parts dried elderberries
- 5 parts mint
- 3 parts tulsi
- 3 parts anise seeds
- 2 parts dried orange zest
- 1 part licorice root

Pour 1.5 cups of hot water on 1 tablespoon of tea mixture. Steep for up to 10 minutes.

108. Protect Yourself from Problems

Ingredients:

- 1 part dried blueberries

- 1 part dried cranberries
- 1 part corn silk
- 1 part Oregon grape root
- 0.5 part nettle leaf
- 0.5 part dandelion leaf
- 0.5 part hibiscus
- 0.5 part uva ursi

Pour 1.5 cups of hot water on 1 tablespoon of tea mixture.
Steep for up to 10 minutes.

109. Protect Your Heart from Attack

Ingredients:

- 1 part hawthorn berry
- 1 part hawthorn leaf
- 1 part linden
- 1 part cinnamon
- 0.5 part lemongrass
- 0.5 part hibiscus

Pour 1.5 cups of hot water on 1 tablespoon of tea mixture.
Steep for up to 10 minutes.

110. Psychic Protection

Ingredients:

- 1 teaspoon lemon balm
- 1 teaspoon peppermint
- 1 teaspoon honey
- 2 sprigs of fresh rosemary
- A few drops of coconut milk

Mix first two ingredients.
Pour 1.5 cups of hot water on 1 tablespoon of tea mixture.
Steep for up to 10 minutes.
Add honey and coconunt milk before serving, garnish with rosemary.

111. Ward Away Negativity

Ingredients:

- 1 teaspoon black tea
- ¼ teaspoon hyssop
- 1 teaspoon honey
- 1 slice lemon

Mix first two ingredients.
Pour 1.5 cups of hot water on 1 tablespoon of tea mixture.
Steep for up to 10 minutes.
Add honey and lemon to cup before serving.

112. Fight Negative Energies

Ingredients:

- 3 parts dandelion root
- 1 part spearmint
- 1 part peppermint
- 1 part fennel
- 1 part ginger
- 0.5 part chamomile

Pour 1.5 cups of hot water on 2 tablespoons of tea mixture.
Steep for up to 15 minutes.

113. Protect your Body and Mind

Ingredients:

- 1 part dandelion root
- 1 part ashwagandha
- 0.5 part gotu kola
- 0.5 part nettle leaf
- 0.5 part peppermint
- 0.25 part licorice root

Pour 1.5 cups of hot water on 2 tablespoons of tea mixture.
Steep for up to 15 minutes.

114. Protect Yourself from Stress and Negativity

Ingredients:

- 2 parts dried cranberries
- 1 part corn silk
- 1 part horsetail
- 1 part nettle leaf
- 0.5 part dandelion leaf

Pour 1.5 cups of hot water on 2 tablespoons of tea mixture.
Steep for up to 15 minutes.

115. Protect Yourself from Black Spells

Ingredients:

- 2 tablespoons grated fresh turmeric
- 2 tablespoons grated fresh ginger
- 2 tablespoons goji berries
- 1/2 teaspoon clove
- 1/2 teaspoon cardamom
- 1 teaspoon honey per cup
- 1 teaspoon black tea per cup

Combine the herbs and spices in a lidded saucepan with 4 cups of water.
Simmer over low heat for about 15 minutes.
Turn it off and add the tea and honey.
Allow to sit for about 5 minutes.

116. Protect Yourself from Dark Spirits

Ingredients:

- 2 parts ginger
- 2 parts milky oat tops
- 2 parts honeybush
- 1.5 parts rose hips
- 1.5 parts lemongrass
- 0.5 part cinnamon
- 0.5 part orange zest

Pour 1.5 cups of hot water on 2 tablespoons of tea mixture.
Steep for up to 15 minutes.

Seasons and Nature

117. Winter Solstice Eve

Ingredients:

- 4 parts honeybush
- 2 parts dried elderberries
- 1 part cedar tips
- 0.5 part whole cloves

Pour 1.5 cups of hot water on 1 tablespoon of tea mixture.
Steep for up to 10 minutes.

118. Winter Spells

Ingredients:

- 2 parts fenugreek seeds
- 2 parts Douglas fir tips
- 1 part cardamom
- 1 part cinnamon
- 1 part ginger
- 0.5 part nutmeg

Pour 1.5 cups of hot water on 1 tablespoon of tea mixture.
Steep for up to 10 minutes.

119. Summer Spells

Ingredients:

- 1 part hawthorn leaf and flower
- 1 part Douglas fir tips
- 1 part anise seeds
- 1 part nettle leaf
- 1 part rose petals

- 1 part mint

Pour 1.5 cups of hot water on 1 tablespoon of tea mixture. Steep for up to 10 minutes.

120. Spring Spells

Ingredients:

- 3 parts nettle leaf
- 1.5 parts peppermint
- 1.5 parts catnip
- 1.5 parts anise seeds
- 1 part marshmallow root
- 1 part elderflower
- 0.5 part red clover blossoms

Pour 1.5 cups of hot water on 1 tablespoon of tea mixture. Steep for up to 10 minutes.

121. Autumn Spells

Ingredients:

- 3 parts burdock root
- 3 parts reishi mushrooms
- 3 parts fennel
- 3 parts dandelion root
- 1.5 parts ginger
- 1 part cinnamon
- 1 part whole cloves
- 1 part astragalus

In a lidded saucepan mix 3 tablespoons tea and 4 cups water. Bring to a simmer and maintain for a minimum of 30 minutes.

122. Honor Mother Nature

Ingredients:

- 5 parts sencha tea
- 2.5 parts milky oat tops
- 1 part red clover blossoms
- 1 part nettle leaf

Pour 1.5 cups of hot water on 1 tablespoon of tea mixture. Steep for up to 10 minutes.

123. Honor Summer's Spirits

Ingredients:

- 4 parts rooibos
- 4 parts dried elderberry
- 4 parts rosehips
- 3 parts rose petals
- 2 parts milky oat tops
- 1 part lavender blossoms
- 1 part calendula flowers
- 1 part lemongrass

Pour 1.5 cups of hot water on 2 tablespoons of tea mixture. Steep for up to 15 minutes.

124. Honor the Northern Spirits

Ingredients:

- 2 teaspoons anise seeds
- 2 teaspoons cinnamon
- 2 tablespoons grated fresh ginger
- 1 teaspoon orange zest
- 1 teaspoon cardamom
- 1 teaspoon crushed clove
- 1 teaspoon rose hips
- 1/2 teaspoon vanilla extract
- 1/2 teaspoon ground nutmeg

In a covered pot, combine 6 to 8 cups of cold red wine and the spices. Heat slowly until steaming, but not boiling. Put on the lowest heat setting and allow the herbs to rest for 20 minutes in the liquid. Keep warm and strain the liquid as you pour each cup.

125. Celebrate the Sun

Ingredients:

- 1 part rose hips
- 1 part Douglas fir tips
- 1 part tulsi
- 0.75 part hibiscus
- 0.5 part calendula flowers

Pour 1.5 cups of hot water on 1 tablespoon of tea mixture.
Steep for up to 10 minutes.

Love and Self Love

126. Embrace Love

Ingredients:

- 2 teaspoons spearmint
- 1 teaspoon angelica root
- 1 teaspoon mugwort
- A bit of rosemary
- 2 star anise

Mix first three ingredients.
Pour 1.5 cups of hot water on 1 tablespoon of tea mixture.
Place 1 star anise and some rosemary in each cup.
Steep for up to 10 minutes.

127. Look and Feel Your Best

Ingredients:

- 2 teaspoons rosehips

- 1 teaspoon blue vervain
- ½ teaspoon anise seed
- 1 teaspoon of honey
- 1 sprig of fresh rosemary

Mix first three ingredients.
Pour 1.5 cups of hot water on 1 tablespoon of tea mixture.
Steep for up to 10 minutes.
Add honey and garnish with rosemary before serving.

128. Attraction

Ingredients:

- 3 teaspoons oolong tea
- 3/8 teaspoon fenugreek seeds
- 6 dried dandelion blossoms
- 3 tiny pieces of ginger

Mix the first two ingredients.
Pour 1.5 cups of hot water mixture
Place 2 dandelions and 1 piece ginger in each cup.
Steep for up to 10 minutes.

129. Broken Heart

Ingredients:

- 1 teaspoon black tea
- 1 teaspoon lavender
- 1 teaspoon white willow bark
- 1 teaspoon mullein
- 1 teaspoon milk thistle
- 1 teaspoon violet blossoms
- 1 star anise
- 2 teaspoons honey

Mix the first six ingredients.
Pour 1.5 cups of hot water on 1 tablespoon of tea mixture.
Add one star anise to each cup.

Steep for up to 10 minutes.
Add honey before serving.

130. Self-Love

Ingredients:

- 1 tablespoon dried strawberries
- 1 teaspoon hibiscus
- 1 teaspoon yarrow
- 1 teaspoon rose petals
- 1 teaspoon brown sugar

Mix the first four ingredients.
Pour 1.5 cups of hot water on 1 tablespoon of tea mixture.
Steep for up to 10 minutes.
Add brown sugar to taste before serving.

131. Love Your Life

Ingredients:

- 1 part chamomile
- 1 part rose petals
- 0.5 part rosehips
- 0.5 part hibiscus
- 1 vanilla bean per pound of tea

Pour 1.5 cups of hot water on 1 tablespoon of tea mixture.
Steep for up to 10 minutes.

132. Attracting True Love

Ingredients:

- 1 part dried ground ginger
- 1 part hibiscus
- 1 part ginseng

Pour 1.5 cups of hot water on 1 tablespoon of tea mixture.

Steep for up to 10 minutes.

133. Increase Sexual Energy

Ingredients:

- 1 teaspoon catnip
- 1 teaspoon ginseng
- 1 teaspoon cinnamon

Pour 1.5 cups of hot water on 1 tablespoon of tea.
Steep for up to 10 minutes.

134. Most Effective Love Potion

Ingredients:

- 1 teaspoon black tea
- 1 teaspoon raspberry leaf
- 1 teaspoon damiana
- 1 teaspoon rosehips
- 1 teaspoon chamomile

Pour 1.5 cups of hot water on 1 tablespoon of tea mixture.
Steep for up to 10 minutes.

135. Love and Protection

Ingredients:

- 1 part eupatorium
- 1 part hyssop
- 1 part red clover
- A pinch of elm

Pour 1.5 cups of hot water on 2 tablespoons of tea mixture.
Steep for up to 15 minutes.

136. Find The One that is Meant for You

Ingredients:

- 5 parts milky oats
- 3 parts damiana
- 2 parts muira puama
- 2 parts siberian ginseng
- 2 parts peppermint
- 2 parts fennel
- 1.5 parts ginger
- 1 vanilla bean per pound of tea
- 1 part rose

Pour 1.5 cups of hot water on 2 tablespoons of tea mixture. Steep for up to 15 minutes.

137. Attract the Right Person for You

Ingredients:

- 2 parts rose hips
- 2 parts dried berries
- 2 parts hibiscus
- 1 part linden
- 1 part lemongrass
- 0.75 part cinnamon

Pour 1.5 cups of hot water on 2 tablespoons of tea mixture. Steep for up to 15 minutes.

138. Finally See the One who Cares about You

Ingredients:

- 3 parts milky oats
- 1 part lemongrass
- 2 parts honeybush
- 2 parts ginger
- 1 part blueberry
- 1 part fennel

- 1 part rose hips

Pour 1.5 cups of hot water on 2 tablespoons of tea mixture. Steep for up to 15 minutes.

139. Stop Pushing Away the One who Loves You

Ingredients:

- 3 parts fenugreek seeds
- 2 parts goji berries
- 2 parts milky oat tops
- 2 parts oat straw
- 2 parts mint
- 1 part nettle leaf
- 1 part alfalfa
- 1 part anise seeds
- 0.5 part safflower
- 0.25 part red clover blossoms

Pour 1.5 cups of hot water on 2 tablespoons of tea mixture. Steep for up to 15 minutes.

140. Be More Confident in Love

Ingredients:

- 3 parts roasted barley
- 1 part astragalus
- 1 part chaga mushrooms
- 0.5 part cinnamon
- 0.5 part burdock root
- 0.5 part star anise

In a lidded saucepan mix 3 tablespoons tea and 4 cups water. Bring to a simmer and maintain for a minimum of 10 minutes.

141. A Night with Someone Special

Ingredients:

- 2 parts raw cacao powder
- 1.5 parts chamomile
- 1 part peppermint
- 1 teaspoon honey
- 0.75 part cinnamon
- 0.35 part star anise
- A little bit of cayenne

In a saucepan, mix 3/4 cup water and 3/4 cup milk. Reduce to low heat. Pour it over up to 2 tablespoons of tea. Steep for up to 10 minutes. Finally, add the honey.

142. Be Surrounded by Friends and Love

Ingredients:

- 1 teaspoon white tea
- 1 teaspoon hibiscus
- 1 teaspoon jasmine
- 1 dash of lemon zest
- 1 teaspoon honey

Brew the zest and flowers for about 4-5 minutes, then add the tea leaves and let it rest 2 more extra minutes. Add the honey at the very end.

Special Recipes

Cold Infusions

143. Say a Wish at Bedtime

Ingredients:

- 1 part mint
- 1 part raspberry leaf
- 1 part nettle leaf
- 0.5 part chamomile
- 0.5 part rose petals

In a lidded jar, mix 2 tablespoons of tea with 3 quarts of water. Refrigerate for a minimum of 2 hours.

144. Honor the Hawaiian Deities

Ingredients:

- 1 part kava root
- 1 part blueberries
- 1 part lemongrass
- 1 part milky oat tops
- 0.75 part fresh ginger
- 0.25 part licorice root

In a lidded jar, mix 2 tablespoons tea with 3 quarts of water. Refrigerate for a minimum of 4 hours and shake from time to time. Strain before using.

145. Abundance in Summertime

Ingredients:

- 2 sprigs fresh mint
- 1 teaspoon green tea
- 1 medium chopped cucumber

- 1 sprig cilantro
- 1 sliced lime
- 1 tablespoon honey
- 1/4 sliced jalapeño

Mix all ingredients and 4 cups of water in a lidded jar. Refrigerate overnight.

146. Achieve Serenity

Ingredients:

- 4 parts milky oat tops
- 1.5 parts elderberry
- 1 part cinnamon
- 1 part linden leaf and flower
- 1 part hawthorn leaf and flower
- 1 part lemongrass
- 1 part fennel

In a lidded jar, mix 2 tablespoons of tea with 4 quarts of water. Refrigerate for a minimum of 3 hours.

147. Ask for a Sweet Desire

Ingredients:

- 2 teaspoons green tea
- 1 cup water
- 1/ 2 cup apple juice
- 2 tablespoons cranberry juice
- 1 teaspoon grated fresh ginger
- 1 handful minced fresh mint
- Zest of 1 lemon

In a lidded jar, mix all ingredients and refrigerate overnight.

148. Refresh Your Soul

Ingredients:

- 1 part jasmine green tea
- 1 part fresh peppermint
- A bit of lime juice

In a lidded jar, mix 2 tablespoons tea and 4 cups water. Refrigerate for a minimum of 3 hours.

149. Summer Wish

Ingredients:

- 2 teaspoons black tea
- 1 cup lemonade
- 1/2 cup water
- A bit of grated fresh ginger

In a lidded jar, mix all ingredients. Refrigerate for a minimum of 3 hours.

Sun Tea Recipes

150. Summer Luck

Ingredients:

- 1 part tulsi
- 0.5 part mint
- 0.5 part hibiscus
- 0.5 part fennel
- 0.5 part raspberry leaf

In a lidded jar, mix 3 tablespoons of tea with 4 quarts of water. Place it in the sun for up to 3 hours and shake from time to time. Strain and add ice if desired.

151. Make a Wish to the Sun

Ingredients:

- 2 cups fresh berries
- 1 ounce dried hibiscus
- 1 handful of fresh mint leaves
- 1 sliced lemon

In a lidded jar, mix all ingredients with 2 quarts of water. Place it in the sun for up to 3 hours and shake from time to time. Strain and add ice if desired.

152. Make Summer Dreams Come True

Ingredients:

- 1 handful of chopped fresh mint
- 1/2 sliced lemon
- 1/4 ounce hibiscus
- 1 sprig fresh rosemary
- A bit of grated, fresh ginger

In a lidded jar, mix all ingredients with 4 quarts of water. Place it in the sun for up to 3 hours and shake from time to time. Strain and add ice if desired.

153. Nurture Your Soul

Ingredients:

- 1 part dried mint
- 1 part nettle leaf
- 1 part dried raspberry leaf
- 0.5 part dried lemon balm
- 0.5 part rose petals

In a lidded jar, mix 3 tablespoons of tea with 4 quarts of water. Place it in the sun for up to 3 hours and shake from time to time. Strain and add ice if desired.

Chai Tea Recipes

154. Inner Elegance (Chai Concentrate)

Ingredients:

- 3 parts dried ginger
- 2 parts fennel seeds
- 1 part cinnamon
- 1 part cardamom
- 0.25 part black pepper

155. Spicy Witches (Chai Concentrate)

Ingredients:

- 1 teaspoon black tea per cup
- 3 parts grated fresh ginger
- 2 parts cinnamon
- 1 part fennel
- 1 part cardamom
- 0.5 part star anise
- 0.25 part clove
- 0.25 part orange zest
- 0.25 part allspice
- 0.1 part black pepper

156.Magic Recipe for Luxurious Dreams (Chai Concentrate)

Ingredients:

- 3.5 parts rooibos
- 3 parts ginger
- 2 parts cardamom
- 2 parts fennel
- 1.5 parts cinnamon
- 0.5 part orange zest
- 0.5 part allspice
- 0.25 part nutmeg

157.For a Sensual Experience (Chai Concentrate)

Ingredients:

- 3 parts Darjeeling tea
- 2 parts grated fresh ginger
- 1 part dried orange zest
- 1 part cardamom
- 1 part cinnamon
- 0.5 part nutmeg
- 0.25 part black pepper
- 1 vanilla bean per pound of blended tea

158. Make the Rain Go Away (Chai Concentrate)

Ingredients:

- 1 teaspoon black tea per cup
- 3 parts grated fresh ginger
- 2 parts cinnamon
- 2 parts fennel
- 1 part cardamom
- 0.5 part nutmeg
- 0.5 part allspice
- 0.5 part clove
- 0.25 part black pepper

159. Bright Future (Chai Concentrate)

Ingredients:

- 3 parts rooibos
- 2 parts dried ginger
- 1 part cinnamon
- 0.5 part cardamom
- 0.5 part star anise
- 0.25 part allspice
- 1 vanilla bean per pound of blended tea

160. Uplift Yourself (Chai Tea)

Ingredients:

- 2 parts black tea
- 1 part fennel
- 1 part mint
- 0.5 part cinnamon
- 0.25 part clove
- 0.25 part cardamom

Pour 1.5 cups of hot water on 1 tablespoon of tea mixture. Steep for up to 8 minutes.

161. Feel Like a Goddess (Chai Tea)

Ingredients:

- 3 parts black tea
- 2 parts cardamom
- 2 parts rose petals
- 1 part mint
- 1 part cinnamon
- 1 vanilla bean per pound of blended tea

Pour 1.5 cups of hot water on 1 tablespoon of tea mixture. Steep for up to 8 minutes.

162. When You're Feeling a Little Low (Iced Chai)

Ingredients:

- 3 parts grated fresh ginger
- 1 part cinnamon
- 1 part fennel
- 0.5 part cardamom
- 0.25 part licorice root
- Sugar
- Black tea

Mix first five ingredients. In a covered pot, combine 1/4 cup spice blend and 5 cups water. Simmer for at least 15 minutes on low heat. Remove the pan from the heat and stir in 2 tablespoons of sugar. Put in the refrigerator to cool. Then, add 4 tablespoons of black tea and continue refrigerating for at least 2 hours.

163. Increase Attraction (Iced Chai)

Ingredients:

- 3 parts ginger
- 2.5 parts cinnamon
- 2.5 parts cardamom
- 2.5 parts fennel
- 2 parts roasted cacao skins
- 2 parts black tea
- 1.5 parts chaga mushrooms

In a lidded jar, mix 2 tablespoons tea and 4 cups water. Refrigerate for a minimum of 2 hours.

Conclusions

I really hope you have enjoyed this book. Tea witchcraft is a fascinating topic, and, of course, there is still so much you can learn about it.

You should know by now that this kind of magic can enhance your life in many different ways. And you will soon discover that your abilities will significantly improve once you start experimenting and preparing recipes that feel right for YOU.

So, embrace this new experience with a confident and open mind, trusting that tea magic will help you achieve your dreams.

And of course, if you want your spells and rituals to be effective, never forget to practice your magic with respect and, above all, for the right reason.

I wish you the best of luck in this magical journey, and if you want to help me spread this information to more people, don't forget to leave your opinion about this book on the corresponding Amazon page:

Together, we can create a more magical world.

Thank you for reading, and... never stop believing!

Alyssa

Made in the USA
Las Vegas, NV
27 July 2023

75327260R00098